DIGITAL PRIVACY

Digital Privacy:
A Guide to Computer Privacy
by M.L. Shannon
Copyright © 1993 by M. L. Shannon
ISBN 0-87364-774-2

Printed in the United States of America
Published by Paladin Press,
a division of Paladin Enterprises, Inc.,
P.O. Box 1307, Boulder, Colorado 80306, USA.
(303) 443-7250

Direct inquiries and/or orders to the above address.

This book contains information that could be used for unlawful purposes. It is not the intent of the author, the publisher, or the seller for it to be used this way, nor do the author or publisher or seller encourage anyone to break existing laws. Neither the author nor the publisher nor the seller will be responsible for the unlawful use of this information, or the consequences thereof, either civil or criminal. If in doubt, consult an attorney.

Digital Privacy is distributed worldwide. Readers in the US are advised that the use of two of the programs reviewed here; PGP, and the Iris public key program, may be in violation of a patent and exclusive rights to certain encryption algorithms owned by RSA Data Security, Inc.

Readers outside the US are advised that the use of encryption programs that were produced in the US may be a violation of US export laws and possibly local laws.

Digital Privacy is for everyone who uses a computer, either at home or on the job, but is oriented towards users rather than programmers and software engineers. Therefore, some of the information about how encryption programs work has been simplified to make it easy to understand. A glossary of terms is included to explain terms that the reader may not be familiar with.

A number of products are mentioned in this book. I have not received, nor will I accept, compensation in any form in exchange for favorably reviewing anything I otherwise would not have. I calls 'em as I sees 'em.

This book was printed in the USA on partially recycled paper. Save a tree.

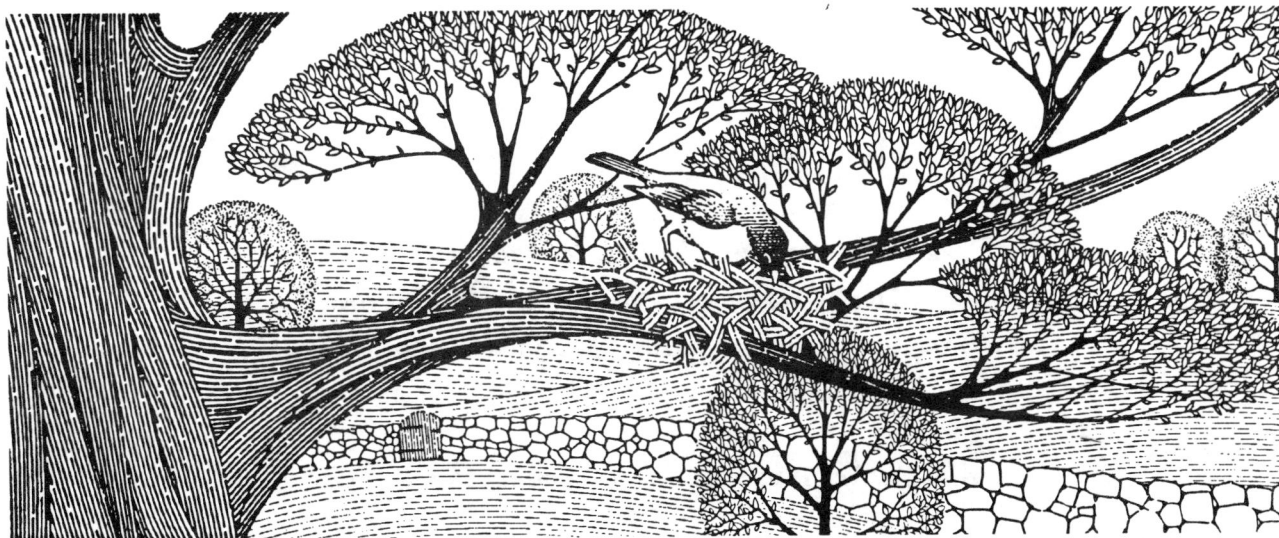

CREDIT WHERE CREDIT IS DUE, AND OTHER STUFF

The reference staff of the San Francisco main library; overworked and understaffed because of budget cuts, they do a fine job.

The University of California at Berkeley for access to their computerized library card catalogue "Violet".

Philip Zimmermann, Kevin Murray of Murray Associates, James Bidzos, President of RSA Data Security, Inc. and 2600 Magazine, for permission to reprint copyrighted material.

The Privacy Project, a series of 13 broadcasts aired on National Public Radio, and produced by Gregg McVicar of Western Public Broadcasting.

These, and others who do not want to be named, have helped make this book possible.

Special thanks to the many people from all over the world who have posted useful information and provided answers to my questions on the Internet.

Other Stuff

Questions, comments, and criticisms are welcomed. All letters will be answered (eventually) but please include a return envelope.

If you read *Don't Bug Me*, you may recall that I mentioned interviewing people at shopping malls and on street corners. I was asking if they knew anything about electronic surveillance. "Oh, well, I never really thought about it" was the most common response. Those who "had thought about it" knew next to nothing about it. They don't want to know. They don't care.

If I were to ask the same people about the security of their home and business computers, I suspect I would get the same answers.

Beside that fact that so many people don't care, or "can't be bothered" with such things there is the limited availability of computer security products. Very few places sell them.

Need an encryption program? Don't look for it at Egghead.

The makers of our Constitution undertook to secure conditions favorable to the pursuit of happiness... They conferred, as against the government, the right to be let alone.

Mr. Justice Brandeis US Supreme Court 1928

DIGITAL PRIVACY CONTENTS

INTRODUCTION

Digital Privacy is about the security of computers and the data they process, store, and sometimes transfer to other computers; it is about how spies, which I call The Datanappers, can steal your computer or invade the privacy of your files; and it is about what you can do to stop them.

Is this book necessary?

I was at an Old English pub last year, celebrating the publishing of my first book, Don't Bug Me, by Paladin Press.

Some guy was looking at the cover, and he sidles up and asks, "What kinda book is that?"

I tell him a little bit about it and he starts getting uptight. When I told him about some of the other books I was working on, he really got hot. "Why you're publishing information that criminals and drug dealers can use to evade the law" he says. "You have no right ..." That was the wrong thing to say. [1]

I got a little hot myself, and told him that I am one of an increasing number of people who are against the way the government is invading our privacy and taking away our rights. I told him about some of the sophisticated equipment that the feds can use to eavesdrop on people's computers; about how the NSA tried to prevent us from having a secure program to encrypt our computer files, and about Operation Sun Devil. I went on and on, and soon a number of people in the pub were listening intently. I ranted on about how the feds are sticking their noses into people's private business by intercepting their electronic mail and how privacy is dying at the hands of government. [2]

I told him about the growing market for stolen computers and how easy it is to steal them, and how the loss of a computer, as well as the data stored in it, can have a devastating effect on peoples lives, and that this happens because people don't know how to protect themselves.

Finally I told him that the books I write are intended to show people how to fight back and defend their right to privacy.

When I finally stopped, several people stood up and cheered. If others were as willing to listen, there would be a lot more privacy and a lot less computer crime in America.

Damn right this book is necessary.

Not The Last Word

Digital Privacy is not intended to be the last word on the subject of computer security. It is intended to show the many ways that computer data is at risk, what tools are available to "The Datanappers", and what tools are available to you, the user, to defeat them. By using the information in this book, you can keep The Datanappers out of your private personal and business files. Not slow them down, not make it difficult for them, *keep them out*.

PART I: DATA ENCRYPTION.

Part one of Digital Privacy is about ciphers; encryption programs that can "scramble" the files on your computer to keep anyone else from reading them. If they are used right, some of them are so effective that no one can reconstruct the files. It is *extremely* unlikely that even the super-secret federal government agencies that We The People know so little about can decrypt them.

Do You Need Data Encryption?

The following article may answer that question for you. It was written by Mr. Phillip Zimmermann, author of Pretty Good Privacy, an encryption program, and is reprinted with his permission.

Why Do You Need PGP?

It's personal. It's private. And it's no one's business but yours.

You may be planning a political campaign, discussing your taxes, or having an illicit affair. Or you may be doing something that you feel shouldn't be illegal, but is.

Whatever it is, you don't want your private electronic mail (E-mail) or confidential documents read by anyone else.

There's nothing wrong with asserting your privacy. Privacy is as apple-pie as the Constitution. Perhaps you think your E-mail is legitimate enough that encryption is unwarranted. If you really are a law-abiding citizen with nothing to hide, then why don't you always send your paper mail on postcards?

Why not submit to drug testing on demand? Why require a warrant for police searches of your house? Are you trying to hide something? You must be a subversive or a drug dealer if you hide your mail inside envelopes. Or maybe a paranoid nut.

Do law-abiding citizens have any need to encrypt their E-mail? What if everyone believed that law-abiding citizens should use postcards for their mail? If some brave soul tried to assert his privacy by using an envelope for his mail, it would draw suspicion. Perhaps the authorities would open his mail to see what he's hiding.

Fortunately, we don't live in that kind of world, because everyone protects most of their mail with envelopes. So no one draws suspicion by asserting their privacy with an envelope. There's safety in numbers. Analogously, it would be nice if everyone routinely used encryption for all their E-mail, innocent or not, so that no one drew suspicion by asserting their E-mail privacy with encryption. Think of it as a form of solidarity.

Today, if the Government wants to violate the privacy of ordinary citizens, it has to expend a certain amount of expense and labor to intercept and steam open and read paper mail, and listen to and possibly transcribe spoken telephone conversation. This kind of labor-intensive monitoring is not practical on a large scale. This is only done in important cases when it seems worthwhile.

More and more of our private communications are being routed through electronic channels. Electronic mail will gradually replace conventional paper mail. E-mail messages are just too easy to intercept and scan for interesting keywords

This can be done easily, routinely, automatically, and undetectably on a grand scale. International cablegrams are already scanned this way on a large scale by the NSA. We are moving toward a future when the nation will be crisscrossed with high capacity fiber optic data networks linking together all our increasingly ubiquitous personal computers

E-mail will be the norm for everyone, not the novelty it is today. Perhaps the Government will protect our E-mail with Government-designed encryption protocols. Probably most people will trust that. But perhaps some people will prefer their own protective measures.

Senate Bill 266, a 1991 omnibus anti-crime bill, had an unsettling measure buried in it.

If this non binding resolution had become real law, it would have forced manufacturers of secure communications equipment to insert special "trap doors" in their products, so that the Government can read anyone's encrypted messages.

It reads: "It is the sense of Congress that providers of electronic communications services and manufacturers of electronic communications service equipment shall insure that communications systems permit the Government to obtain the plain text contents of voice, data, and other communications when appropriately authorized by law."

This measure was defeated after rigorous protest from civil libertarians and industry groups. But the Government has since introduced other disturbing legislation to work toward similar objectives.

If privacy is outlawed, only outlaws will have privacy.

Intelligence agencies have access to good cryptographic technology. So do the big arms and drug traffickers. So do defense contractors, oil companies, and other corporate giants.

But ordinary people and grassroots political organizations mostly have not had access to affordable "military grade" public-key cryptographic technology. Until now. PGP empowers people to take their privacy into their own hands. There's a growing social need for it. That's why I wrote it.

It seems that Mr. Zimmermann makes a Pretty Good Argument. The Senate bill that he refers to (SB 266) is just one example of how the government has tried to take away our privacy and the right to be left alone.

The "PGP" that he refers to is one of several data encryption programs that are available to We The People. In Digital Privacy, you can learn about them, and other ways of keeping your private information private. It is interesting how all this came to be, so before we get into ciphers, lets look back in time...

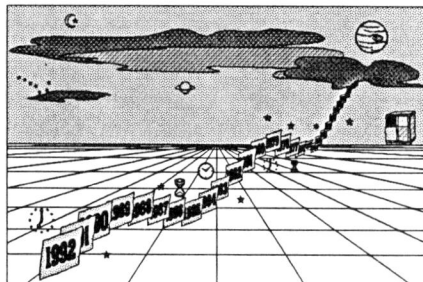

A HISTORY OF COMPUTERS

Personal computers have been available for only about 20 years. Before that, there were only the mainframe systems used by big businesses and government. Some of the earliest of them were the Univac, the Eniac, and Colossus. The Colossus was built by the British in about 1943 apparently to break the German Enigma ciphering machine. Possibly the very first electronic computer was, according to Bamford's *Puzzle Palace,* the Bronze Goddess, built in 1940, also by the British. It was also used to break the Enigma.

The Tube

These early systems were very expensive, some occupied large rooms, and used vacuum tubes, thousands of them. One system, built for the U.S. Air Force supposedly used 50,000.

Where the computers of today are digital, the early ones were analog. They were unpredictable and were attended by teams of technicians and engineers who were frequently swarming over them, tinkering and adjusting things, and of course replacing burned out tubes. As big and as complex as they were, they didn't have the computational power of some of today's scientific pocket calculators. But, they were a beginning.

The Transistor

In December 1947 the transistor was invented at Bell Labs by Drs. Bardeen, Brattain, and Shockley. This was one of the greatest advances in electronics; it was to change the world, but like any new invention, much was to be done before it was ready to market. Besides setting up facilities to mass produce and package it, there were a lot of improvements to be made. These early transistors didn't switch (work) as fast as vacuum tubes, so they weren't able to operate at high frequencies, and they could handle only very small amounts of power. So for some years, while transistors were being improved to overcome these limitations, "hybrids" were developed. Two way radios, for example, used transistors in the audio stages and tubes in the RF sections.

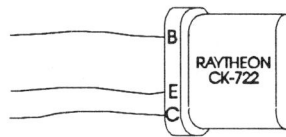

In the early fifties the first transistor for consumer sale was released. This was the Raytheon CK-722, which sometimes included a little booklet of diagrams on how to build a portable radio, and other projects. In about 1956, one of the very first all transistor consumer products went on sale. It was a pocket size AM radio called the Zenith Royal 500 and it cost about $175.00, a princely sum back in the days when fifty dollars worth of groceries took two hands to carry.

In a few years, many of these problems of transistors were worked out. They became smaller and faster, and able to handle larger amounts of power, and because of the size and low power drain, they soon replaced the vacuum tubes in computers. Another revolution in the computer industry, but it created yet another new problem. So small did they become that connecting thousands of them together became more and more difficult. So many wires in so small a space made this a very tedious process, and someone came up with the expression "tyranny of numbers"

There had to be a better way, so someone came up with the idea of placing a number of individual transistors inside one small package, which became the integrated circuit. The first one had only three, and cost close to a thousand dollars to produce. Compare that with some of the chips of today, which contain thousands of transistors and can be bought for a few cents.

Satellites & Atom Bombs

All of this had to happen, in the natural way that things evolve, but possibly the one single event that most influenced the development of smaller and more powerful computers came in 1957. In October of that year, the world's first orbiting satellite, Sputnik, was launched by the Soviet Union.

This was at the height of the cold war with "Them Russians". It was a time when "Better Dead Than Red" bumper stickers were seen on many a vehicle, the FBI was out beating the bushes for "commies", and families spent week-ends shopping for fallout shelters.

Sputnik had Americans rather concerned. People were talking and speculating about what this man made satellite could do. Some seriously believed that it contained "An Atom Bomb" that could be dropped on us any time the Russians wanted.

Others believed that Sputnik could spy on them; hear what they were saying and watch what they were doing. As we now know, it could do none of these things. Unlike some of the satellites of today. which can read a license plate or newspaper headline from 12,000 miles up, Sputnik was completely harmless.

However, it did a lot to get this country into action and the space race began. "Keep up with the Russians."

A few years later, President Kennedy decided that we should "land a man on the moon and return him safely to earth"

Now flying to the moon in a rocket is a rather complicated operation. A great many calculations have to be made to navigate the ship, as well as monitor onboard conditions such as fuel flow and oxygen consumption, and

handle communications with planet Earth. Only a computer could do the job, but the systems that were capable of this were too big and consumed far too much power to be used aboard a moon rocket.

So the government and scientific community got to work, and a few years later, Alan Shepard orbited the Earth and Neil Armstrong became the first human to set foot on the moon.

From that technology home computers evolved. It was another one of those things that had to happen.

One of the first was the MITS Altair 8800, which was about the size of the proverbial bread box. It didn't have a keyboard; data was entered in assembly language one byte at a time by setting a series of panel switches to the off and on positions for the 8 bits. The display was a set of LED's, rather than a monitor, and it had a whopping 256 bytes of memory.

> *Should you have one of these old Altairs gathering dust in your attic, you might like to know that they are worth a fair amount to collectors.*

Red Apples, Big Blue, & Green Acres

Another revolution in the computer industry came in the seventies; the Apple II and the IBM PC hit the market. They had keyboards and monitors and disk drives, and the era of home computing was born. Two rumors about Apple and IBM: IBM supposedly got the name Big Blue because of the dress code; male employees were required to wear suits, which presumably were blue. The name Apple was coined by Mr. Steve Wozniak; he and several other of the founders were discussing a company name and Woz, observing that one of the others was eating an apple said, "If you don't come up with something, I'm gonna call it the Apple Computing Company".

At any rate, soon everyone was buying them and they even became something of a status symbol. "My computer is bigger than yours..." (And later, "My computer is smaller than yours...) The whole family got involved; for once everyone did something together, other than watch the boob tube.

The kids could play games and maybe even do their homework; dad could balance the checkbook and mother could keep track of her recipes and finish balancing the checkbook that dad screwed up.

This lasted for a few years, but soon the novelty wore off as people began to realize that computers weren't as easy to use as they first thought. Sales went down, and some people thought this was the end of the personal computer market.

The used computer market was created, and many an Apple II or PC could be had at garage sales after their former users gave up and went back to reruns of Green Acres.

However, for small businesses, the self employed and other serious users, personal computers soon became indispensable.

The amount of software available, which was rather sparse in the early days, increased dramatically. Soon there were word processors and databases and spread sheets available, that actually worked.

While this made it easier to process large amounts of information, it also made it easier for others to access, and since some of it was confidential, there was a need to control who could use the system.

For the government, this wasn't a problem. They could control access to their computers with platoons of soldiers with machine guns, attack dogs, and electrified fences. For some businesses though, this was a bit of overkill. It was too much trouble and expense, besides which it might scare the customers away.

The government also had sophisticated data encryption programs that ran on their big mainframe systems, but there weren't any commercially made encryption programs that would work on personal computers. So a number of programmers working independently or sometimes together, began to write programs that were based on some of the paper and pencil encryption methods described below.

In the seventies the Data Encryption Standard was developed, and later it became available to the public to use on their home computers. This was not the happiest day in history for the some of the federal government's spy agencies. Secrets are to be reserved for them alone, and never for We The People. They have tried to prevent this from happening again. [2.5]

There are now many such programs, that provide varying degrees of security, from modest to virtually unbreakable, and costing from nothing to hundreds of dollars. A few of them are described here, some briefly, some in more detail. In a later section some of them are reviewed. For additional sources of information, a few books on cryptology are listed in the bibliography.

A HISTORY OF CIPHERS

In every civilization, from the dawn of recorded history to the present, the strong, the rich and powerful, have controlled and exploited those of the "lower classes", and for thousands of years even had absolute power of life or death over them.

One of the ways the few have maintained control over the many is through forced ignorance.

For hundreds of years the poor, the working class, were forbidden to be able to read and write. Sometimes having this knowledge, or even owning a book, was punishable by torture and execution.

However, even the all powerful church-state could not keep the people ignorant forever, and as they developed reading skills, these written secrets became at risk.

Something had to be done so that this information did not fall into the "wrong" hands. From this need, codes were developed. And broken. New and better codes were devised. And broken. And so began the eternal war between the codemakers and the codebreakers.

One of the earliest examples is the Roman "Caesar Cipher" which was devised by the Emperor himself. It is a simple substitution of one letter for another, in this case the third; A=D, B=E, C=F etc. This is similar to the method used in cryptograms in the newspapers. [3]

Simple, but it worked. Slaves and servants who cooked for and cleaned up after Roman Citizens could not decipher the notes they found in kitchen and dungeon. They had no way of knowing who was to peel the grapes at the next orgy, or who was to satisfy the appetite of the lions.

Some of these old letter substitution ciphers had interesting and colorful names, such as the Russian "Nihilist" and "Prisoners" codes, the "Corkscrew", "Rail Fence", "Spaghetti" and "Swinging Squares".

Another clever idea was the "Spartan Code" The secret information was written on a strip of cloth wound around a certain size spear, then removed. Only by rewrapping it on the same size spear could it be deciphered.

An improvement on the Spartan Code was the French "Bazeries" cipher, which was a code wheel system. In America, Ben Franklin devised one of these code wheels which was quite sophisticated in his time, and during World War II the Germans used the Enigma Machine which was a very sophisticated elaboration of the code wheel.

All of these encryption methods were developed before computers were available. Now that they are, the ongoing war between the code makers and the code breakers has begun a new era. Faster computers could break older codes, but they could also create more complex codes that the same computers could not break. And the war goes on.

The Playfair grid.

I	H	G	F	E
J	V	U	T	D
K	W	Z	S	C
L	X	Y	R	B
M	N	O	P	A

WHAT IS A CIPHER?

The word *cipher*, as well as *algorithm* and *encryption method* refer to any of a number of ways to convert or re-arrange or scramble the text of a document into a form that is unreadable to anyone who does not have a way to convert or re-arrange it back to its original form.

The original, readable, form is called *plaintext* and the encrypted or scrambled form is called *ciphertext*.

This *way*, or method, is usually called a *key* or *password*; the process of scrambling the information is called *encryption*, and the process of converting it back to a readable form is called *decryption*.

Besides using the key to access this information, there are a number of other methods that may work. Analyzing the scrambled information and attempting to convert it back to plaintext without having the key is called *cryptanalysis* and the overall process of trying to do this is called an *attack*. There are several methods of attacking a cipher, or the information encrypted with a cipher.

Later in this book will be the details of these methods of attack and how successful they might be, as well as some other ways a code might be broken.

First, though, a few words about the types of ciphers used in the days before computers.

In the domed cities of the future, there will be little personal privacy. All communications will be controlled and monitored by the government. Cryptography will have been outlawed for the common people.

TYPES OF CIPHERS

The Vigenere

The Vigenere cipher was devised by Blaise de Vigenere in the 1500's, and is a variation on the Caesar cipher. It uses more than one letter substitution; or rather, it uses a method of substitution that changes back and forth. The 26 letters were laid out in a certain pattern known only to the sender and recipient. The keyboard on a typewriter is an example of how it might be done today.

To encrypt a message, one can shift the letters to the right one key for the first letter, two keys for the second letter, and three for the third letter etc.

If the word *tiger* were so encrypted, the T would move one key to Y, the I would move two keys and become P, the G would move three keys to become K, and etc, so tiger becomes "ypkuo".

Rather than the 1,2,3 method, a *key* could be used; a word that is easy to remember. If the key were "VIXEN" for example, then the first letter of the message would be offset by 22, as 'V' is the 22nd letter of the alphabet; the second letter would be offset by 9, 'I' being the ninth letter, etc. Letters that went past Z would continue on around starting again at A.

When all five letters had been used, the process would repeat. To make it even harder to break, thele tters could beput ingro upsof five! like the military once used in radio teletype messages.

The Vernam

The Vernam is a fast cipher, once used to scramble teletype messages. The information was input on punched paper tape, and a second tape was used, synchronized with the first, which used "exclusive or" logic.

The Playfair

The Playfair cipher is another letter substitution cipher, but it differs from the previous examples in that it uses a grid of squares, 5 by 5. Each of the 25 spaces contains one letter of the alphabet. In this example, the letters start with A at the bottom right corner, and continue around in a left hand spiral. The arrangement can be any way one wants to make it.

As there are 26 letters, one is unused, such as Q or J, the loss of which would not effectively change the message content. The letters are then transposed 2 at a time: If the first two letters of the message to be encrypted are in the same row in the grid, the letters to be substituted for them will be those two letters one column to the right. If they are in the same column, the letters to be substituted will be one square towards the bottom of the grid.

For example, the same row letters I and G become H and F; and the samecolumn letters F and Q become S and P.

For letters that are not in the same row or column, use them as the corners of a grid within the grid. The letters E and Y become two of the corners of a grid made up of the 9 letters in the top right corner of the Playfair grid. The letters in the opposite corners are G and C. So E becomes G, and Y becomes C.

The Bazeries

The Bazeries, mentioned above, was a code wheel algorithm. It used a series of 20 wheels, which rotated independently on a shaft; each with the 26 letters of the alphabet engraved on them.

The wheels could be offset a certain, prearranged, number of positions (letters) and the encrypted message would then be in blocks of 20 letters,

The Iris disk listed below includes a computer simulation of the Bazeries encryption program, but it is much more complex. It has 23 "wheels", each with 256 positions, so the entire ASCII character set can be used. A much more secure method, but still breakable by fast computers.

The Enigma

Probably the greatest and most secure of all pre-computer encryption methods is the Enigma machine. The Enigma is a mechanical encryption device that used wheels like the Bazeries, but is much more complex. It was developed in Germany in the 1920's, and sold to businesses and industry. Later, a more secure version was developed for the German Wehrmacht, the military forces.

Both the British and American intelligence agencies were aware of Enigma, and were trying desperately to break the encrypted messages it generated. It was known to the Allies that the war in Europe was coming long before Hitler invaded Poland in 1939, and since the German forces would presumably be using Enigma for military communications it was imperative that it be cracked.

The Enigma machine looks something like an old portable typewriter with 26 keys for the letters of the alphabet, and above the keyboard, a set of 26 small lights, one for each letter. Above the lamps are two rows of jacks that could be cross connected to each other with plugs and wires. Inside the Enigma machine are a number (3 to 8) of individually rotating drums. On each drum is a ring engraved with the letters of the alphabet.

When a key is pushed, the drums rotate in a prearranged and complicated sequence, and select the letter that is to be substituted for the one that was on the key that was pushed. This causes the lamp for that letter to light. Then that letter can be typed on a typewriter or hand written.

Four different factors are involved in setting the key; the order of the rotors, the ring settings, the rotor starting positions, and the arrangement of the plug board connections.

Using three drums, the 26 letters can be arranged in any of 17,576 combinations (26 cubed), and as the order of the drums can be changed, this makes for about 105,000 possible arrangements. Very formidable in the forties when decryption was done with paper and pencil.

Add to that the different arrangements of the plug board connections and it is vastly more complex. Some Enigma machines had 8 drums, which, according to the documentation of the Enigma computer program, made the possible arrangements of letters something like $403 \times 10\,\char94 26$.

It was finally broken by British Military Intelligence at Bletchley Park. This took several years; so cleverly was the Enigma designed it took into consideration patterns, and frequency of letters.

For a fascinating account of Enigma, written by one of the people who was involved in breaking it, see *The Hut Six Story* by Gordon Welchman, McGraw-Hill, 1982

A shareware computer simulation of the Enigma machine is available on some computer bulletin boards; the filename is ENIGMA_2.ZIP. It is interesting to make up secret messages and encrypt them with this program, while picturing a frantic German soldier punching the keys of his Enigma machine as Russian artillery shells are pounding Berlin into rubble in late April 1945. The final days of Hitler's "Thousand Year Reich"

THE RSA AND DES ALGORITHMS.

These ciphers are of historical interest and fun to play with, but being part of the pre-computer age of encryption they will not withstand attack by present technology.

Today, we have a new generation of encryption algorithms, and a different kind of war between those who encrypt and those who try to decrypt. Or sometimes do decrypt.

Where the first generation of codebreakers spent long hours with paper and pencil, painstakingly comparing messages and looking for similarities and letter frequencies, the codebreakers of today are highly skilled mathematicians and programmers. The paper and pencil and the Banbury Sheets of the Enigma era, have been replaced by the fastest and most powerful computers available; the number crunching Crays, and custom made machines developed specifically for breaking the sophisticated ciphers of the 20th century.

Two of these ciphers are the RSA Public Key System and the Data Encryption Standard (DES). They are very secure, and are *resistant* to attack by even these supercomputers.

Information on them will be in two parts, first the RSA public key system, then the Data Encryption Standard.

RSA Programs

In this book, I will provide information on three programs that use the RSA public key algorithm. They are:

MailSafe

MailSafe is a commercial program produced by RSA Data Security, Inc. This program includes the Digital Envelope and the Digital Signature, used for message authentication. It also has a number of other useful features including local encryption and methods of key management.

IRIS

Iris is a shareware program produced in England. The program disk includes the public key, and a number of other programs and utilities. Some of these are the DES, the Playfair, the Vernam, the Littlewood, and the Bazeries ciphers. It is named after the messenger of the gods in Greek mythology. In Greek, Iris means rainbow.

Pretty Good Privacy

Pretty Good Privacy (PGP) is a free public key program written by Philip Zimmermann. It includes a message authentication feature, and a very informative documentation file.

In a business or government environment, there are certain people who have access to confidential data, and others who do not. Or at least aren't supposed to. Often such information has to be sent, in encrypted form, to a distant location over phone lines or by messenger. At these remote places, again, some people have to have the keys needed to decrypt it, and others do not.

With a conventional algorithm, a single key is used to both encrypt and decrypt this information. This can be a problem; as the key is passed around from one authorized person to another, or delivered to other locations, there is always the chance it might fall into the hands of someone who is not authorized to have it. Such as a spy from a foreign country or a competitive company or law firm.

One solution to this problem is the public key algorithm.

The idea of such a system was first devised by Whitfield Diffie and Martin Helman and published in 1976. [4] This was, I understand, based on the work of a scientist named Merkle who devised something called the "knapsack" cipher.

A year later the first workable public key system was developed by Drs. Rivest, Shamir, & Adleman, at the Massachusetts Institute of Technology. It was financed in part, by a grant from the National Science Foundation, is named RSA from the first letters of their last names, and was issued patent number 4,405,829.

Where conventional encryption algorithms use a single key or password, the public key system uses two.

The first of these is the "public key" which can be made available to others. The second is the "private key" which the user keeps secret. If someone wants to send a secret message to someone else, they use that persons public key. Only the recipient can unscramble it by using their private key, so the problem of key distribution is eliminated. Almost. Read on...

Given this, you might consider that it could work in reverse, which it can. If the user encrypts a message with his private key, then only his (and no one else's) public key can decrypt it back into plain text. Clever, no?

How the Public Key System Works.

First we have to create the keys. To do this, we start with some numbers and apply them to the formulas below. Once they are calculated we can use them to encrypt a few "secret messages". The numbers used in this example are:

P which will be 3
Q which will be 11
N which will be 33
D which will be 7
E which will be 3
A which will be 2
B which will be 10
C which will be 20

A is part of the formula used below; P (3) - 1 = 2

B is part of the formula used below; Q (11) - 1 = 10

C is part of the formula used below; [P - 1] * [Q - 1] = 2 * 10 = 20.

The first step in calculating the two keys is to find the number that will be used as N.

Formula: $N = P * Q$

To find N we will select, at random, two prime numbers; which we will call P and Q.

A prime is a number that can be evenly divided by only that number and 1. Seven is prime because it can be evenly divided only by 7 and 1. An example of a non-prime number is 8. It can be evenly divided by 1 and 8, and also 2 and 4.

For this example, we can use 3 for P and 11 for Q.

Now, per the formula, we multiply P times Q which is 33.

The number used for N will be 33.

Second step, find D:

Formula: $D = RP$ to [P-1] * [Q-1] (RP = relatively prime)

For D we need a number that is RP to the formula [P-1] times [Q-1].

From the first step, we know that P = 3 and Q = 11.

[P - 1 = 2] and [Q - 1 = 10].

2 times 10 = 20.

A number that is RP to 20 is 7, so we can use 7 as D.

Third step, find E:

Formula: **[E*D] mod ((P-1) * (Q-1)) = 1.**

Let us break this into smaller parts.

We already know that [P-1] times [Q-1] = 20.

We already know that D is 7.

For E, we need a number that can be multiplied by D (7), then divided by 20 [P-1 * Q-1] so that the remainder is 1.

Such a number is 3.

If we multiply 3 by 7 [E * D] we get 21.

Now 21 mod 20 leaves a remainder of 1 which is what we need. As you can see, mod or modulo, means remainder on division.

The three numbers we have calculated are: N = 33, D = 7, and E = 3

The two keys are [N and D] and [N and E]. If you were using these numbers as your keys you would say "My public key is 3 & 33" [E and N] and (you wouldn't say) "My private key is 7 & 33" [D and N].

Now, let us use these keys and do a sample encryption. The RSA is a number encryption algorithm, so the letters of the secret message will be represented by numbers. More on this below.

To make it easy, we will use a single number. The "secret message" will be the number 4, and the key will be 3 and 33.

First step: We raise the 4 to the 3rd power. The reason it is to the 3rd power is that 3 is the first part of the key.

Four ^3 = 64.

Second step: We calculate 64 modulo 33.

Divide 64 by 33 and the remainder is 31.

The secret message 4 has been encrypted to become 31.

Then we send the 31 to the person who has the private key 7 and 33.

When they get the 31 they raise it to the 7th power, as 7 is the first number of their private key.

Raised to the 7th power, 31 becomes 27512614111.   ·

Then they calculate 27512614111 modulo 33 and the result is 4, the number we started with.

Another example. Let's use the number 5 as the message and the same key, 3 and 33.

First, raise 5 to the 3rd power which is 125.

Second, 125 mod 33 = 26.

To decrypt the 26:

First, 26 to the 7th = 8031810176
Second, 8031810176 mod 33 = 5.

Now lets reverse the process and switch keys. This time we will encrypt with 7 and 33 and decrypt with 3 and 33.

Using the secret message number 5:

Raise 5 to the ^7th we get 78125
78125 mod 33 = 14.

14 is the secret message.

Now to decrypt the 14:
4 raised to the 3rd = 2744
2744 mod 33 = 5

These examples show how the keys are calculated and used, but in an RSA program they are generated automatically by the computer. Also, there are some variations in how they are used in an actual program, which are slightly different than our simplified example. Some RSA programs implement something called the Chinese Remainder theorem, which speeds up the process, and the selection of some of the numbers used to calculate the keys is a little more complicated.

Here is how one generates a pair of keys with the Iris public key program.

From the command line the user types in the following:

GENKEY /KEYLENGTH = 108 /KEYNAME = UNITY2 /KEYFILE = MYKEY

GENKEY is the command used to tell the program to generate the key.

KEYLENGTH = 108 means the key I am about to generate is 108 digits in length. Actually, because of the mechanics of the program, the keys will not be *exactly* 108 digits.

KEYNAME = UNITY2 is the name I am using for this key, so I can tell it from other keys.

KEYFILE = MYKEY tells Iris where to save this key; which file to store them in.

Now the program asks you to type in a series of non-repeating digits with which to calculate the key. When you have entered the right number of them, the program will beep to let you know. In this example I just typed in 1 through 9 over and over.

Enter P0 seed: 1234567890...
Enter P2 seed: 1234567890...
Enter Q0 seed: 1234567890...
Enter Q2 seed: 1234567890...
Enter E seed: 1234567890...

The result is these three long numbers.

[RSA][UNITY2][][Fri Aug 21 12:36:28 1992]

N:
[23230572429426165896013262246044452 7737005259011348972345321345333126 25623753675395287148522441801984777 75353952871485224 4180198477753]

D:
[77435241431420552986710874153481759 1233508633711632309900186182658334 53110034773074699336768045824870007 07307469933676804 5824870007]

E:
[60094567359829160765565195468597810 2281159024255921646181014081528663 858691462747093415098157098901666 43470934150981570 9890166643]

In our first example, it would not be difficult to derive one key from the other. With long numbers like these, it is very difficult. With very long numbers it is not possible.

Fortunately, in the RSA program, it is not necessary to use the keys in this digit form. Typing in these long strings of digits would not only take too much time, but would inevitably result in errors, which could cause you to lose your data. The keys are applied in a much easier form, as will be explained below.

In the above example, it is noted that the RSA is a number encryption system; it scrambles numbers. The message to be encrypted becomes one enormous integer (in ASCII form) that is broken up into small blocks, based on the length of the key.

The following description is from Mr. Moreton, producer of Iris.

"In the RSA, the message to be encrypted is first converted into ASCII. "Its all Greek" becomes 7384833265767632718269." In ASCII, I is 73; T is 84, etc. The message becomes one enormous integer which is encrypted in smaller blocks that are based on the length of the key being used. Imagine, if you will, that the "secret message" were 250 digits long, as compared to the single digit '5' in our example. Then consider that the power it has to be raised to. Even though the principle is simple, processing these huge integers requires some heavy number crunching.

The approximate number of different 150 digit keys available has an exponent of greater than 200. Consider that the distance light can travel, moving at 186,200 miles per second for a million years, has an exponent of 18. Numbers with exponents that big are beyond comprehension to all but mathematicians and the Treasury Department.

Using this method of encryption is slow compared to some other ciphers; perhaps, but not necessarily, too slow for commercial use. So to speed up the process, and still be able to use the public/private key system, the "secret message" can be encrypted with a different, faster, algorithm. Then the key used for this algorithm can be encrypted and decrypted with the RSA keys.

To do this, MailSafe uses the Data Encryption Standard cipher and PGP uses the IDEA cipher. Iris is different in that it does not use a different cipher; it uses the RSA for the actual message encryption. While it isn't as fast, it is the most secure. Unbreakable with present technology. More on this.

Here is an example of sending and receiving a secret message, as it is done with MailSafe. The process is in four parts; **sign**, **seal**, **open**, and **verify**.

The RSA Digital Envelope

Suppose "Alice" decides to send a secret message to "Bob". (Maybe she doesn't want Bob's wife to read it) First she encrypts the message with the DES, using a random one time only, DES key. Then she uses Bob's public key to encrypt that one time only DES key. [5]

The secret message that was encrypted with the DES, and the DES key that was encrypted with Bob's public key, are combined and **sealed** in the *Digital Envelope* which is then sent to Bob.

When Bob receives it, he uses his private key to **open** the envelope; that is to decrypt the DES key. When he has the DES key, he can use it to decrypt the secret message.

If Bob's private key can *decrypt* the DES key, then only Bob's public key could have been used to *encrypt* the DES key.

The RSA Digital Signature

While the secret message is being sent from one location to another, it is possible that it could be changed because of transmission errors (line noise) or tampering. While sometimes there is little that can be done to prevent this, there is a positive way to determine if the message has, in fact, been changed. This is the Digital Signature.

To use it, Alice selects **sign** from the Mail-Safe menu. This feature uses a *hashing algorithm* to create a *message digest*. Then she uses her private key to encrypt this message digest which creates the digital signature. When this is done, she sends it along with the original secret message to Bob (who's wife is starting to get suspicious).

The message digest is a 128 bit string that is like a serial number, or a fingerprint; no two are alike. It is based on the original secret love letter, uh, that is, the confidential business communication. If any part of the original message is changed, even one bit, the message digest will be changed substantially.

When Bob receives the secret message, he again uses the open function to open the envelope that Alice sealed with his public key. Then he can use the same hashing algorithm to create a new message digest based on the received message, and compare it with the one he received to **verify** that they are identical (that the message has not been changed) and to verify Alice's digital signature. The Digital Signature is, according to RSA Data Security, impossible to forge, so it positively identifies the person who sent the message.

The Message Digest can be viewed with the "special function" feature in the MailSafe Utilities menu. If two certain files are supposed to be identical, you can bring up this string of characters and compare them. Two people can do this from different locations via electronic mail or telephone.

With the MailSafe program, all of this is transparent to the user. Being completely menu driven, they can simply follow the prompts without having to type in complicated command line instructions.

PUBLIC KEY MANAGEMENT

When I first heard of the public key system, I visualized huge telephone book size directories of peoples public keys. Fascinating, I thought; it would have keys for all manner of people, whom I could secretly communicate with. Well, not quite.

Now obviously if you are going to send secret messages to people, you have to have their public keys, but they aren't necessarily *that* public. How, and to whom, an individual distributes their public key is up to them. If you obtain a persons public key from such a directory, or any source other than directly from that person, how do you know it really is *their* key?

In some situations, such as a LAN or multi-user system, a number of people have access to the Email and public key files. It is possible for one person to generate a set of keys and substitute the public key in place of the real public key of some unsuspecting person. Another way for this to happen would be on a public access BBS where people list their public keys. If someone were to get sysop access, they could substitute the keys.

> *Suppose you want to use a public key program on a personal computer that others have access to. One copy of MailSafe can be used by a number of different users. The password system prevents one person from accessing another persons private key, or files they encrypted.*

If Bob's wife were able to secretly substitute her public key in place of Alice's, she would be able to read the secret messages Bob was sending to Alice.

She could also change, edit, the messages and encrypt them with Bob's public key, and then put Alice's real key back where it was. This switching of keys could be done with a purchase order, and someone could steal a shipment of widgets, or whatever else, by changing the delivery address.

One way to eliminate this problem is to exchange public keys with others in person, or through a trusted medium. Nike Net. Courier. Armored car. Another is to use Public Key Certification. This is a method of adding a special signature to a key. Certification can be done in two ways; Direct and Extended.

In the direct method, one person certifies another persons key, and vice versa; Bob could certify Alice's key and Alice could certify Bob's key. In the extended method, a trusted third person such as a network administrator certifies the keys of others. The keeper of the keys... In a controlled situation, where all of the keys are kept in a single repository, this eliminates the possibility of keys being switched.

If you plan on using a public key program on a shared system or network, the MailSafe manual will provide the information you need.

THE DATA ENCRYPTION STANDARD

The DES began life as "Project Lucifer"; developed at the IBM research lab in Yorktown, NY. Completed in 1971, its first application was in an early version of the 24 hour teller machine.

Over the next few years, this cipher was re-written and improved (with some help from the NSA) and the National Bureau of Standards (now the National Institute of Standards and Technology, or NIST) became interested in it. This was about the same time the new Lucifer was ready to market; it was built into a chip, and used a 128 bit key. Apparently because of the NSA, IBM "mysteriously" changed the key to 56 bits before they gave it to the NBS.

Why 56?

There are a number of theories about this.

One rumor is that the NSA had the DES developed so that only they could break it, and at 128 bits this was not possible. Another is that at 128 bits the DES ran too slow to process the massive amount of information that government spy agencies have to work with.

I tried calling IBM to see what I could find out, but was never able to find anyone who could (or would) provide me with the information I wanted. (I suspect this was because I was not able to find the right department or division or whatever, rather than IBM being unwilling to talk to me.)

So I posed the question on the Internet newsgroup sci.crypt.

Q4: **Does anyone know why the key was really changed to 56 bits?**

Here are some of the answers I got.

*Much later it has been proven that longer keys don't increase the security of this en-

cryption method. Probably NSA knew that at the time when the algorithm has been designed.

*The reason one usually hears is that was cheaper (DES was intended for hardware implementation, and it was designed in the mid-70s).

*Yes. Unfortunately, it's still classified, and they aren't going to tell us their reasons. However, researchers (Shamir and students) have discovered an attack that allows DES with a key longer than 56 bits to be cracked with the same effort as a 56 bit key. Therefore, a key longer than 56 bits would not have been any more secure. It would be a fair guess to assume that is part, if not all, of the reason for the shortening of the key to 56 bits.

*No. I suppose NSA forced IBM to reduce the keyspace of Lucifer which was 768 bits to a keyspace of 56 bits to protect their own interests.

*"Know"? No one who's talking. My own guess is that it was felt that the intrinsic strength of DES was on the order of 56 bits. A longer key, with everything else held the same except for the key schedule algorithm, could actually be weaker in some ways. The only thing known for sure about longer keys is that they guard against brute force.

*I believe it was system considerations They were working with an eight byte blocksize and wanted a parity check on encrypted keys.

*Someone does. From what we know, DES can't even support 56 bits, if you attack it with Differential Cryptanalysis.

Now you know as much as almost anyone else.

As mentioned in one of the above answers, and in one of the NIST FIPS publications, the DES was originally in hardware form; a chip. In such form, it can not be modified, and also runs faster than in software.

The software versions of the DES could, theoretically, be changed, modified, to include a trap door, or other secret way of decrypting messages encrypted with them. To prevent this, the DES has a compliance test that checks it to make sure it is running as it is supposed to, and has not been modified. See *compliance test*, below.

The Private Line, SuperCrypt and Iris have this test.

> *If you have any doubts about any encryption program, have it examined by a trusted programmer or cryptographer before you use it to protect your confidential data.*

How The DES Works.

Though the key was changed to 56 bits, the DES still works with 64 bit (8 character) blocks. The remaining 8 bits are used for parity, a method of error checking.

The mechanics of the program are complicated, and also depend on which of the four modes is being used. For details on this process of transposing, XORing, and substituting bits, refer to the bibliography which lists books that explain it in technical detail. A simplified explanation:

The DES can work in four different modes; Electronic Code book (ECB), Cipher Feedback (CFB), Cipher Block Chaining (CBC) or Output Feedback (OFB).

The ECB mode is the least secure; each block (8 characters) of the text is encrypted the same way, independently of the others, and can be individually analyzed and compared to the other encrypted blocks.

CBC is the most secure of the four. The CBC mode uses a second number (key) called an "initialization vector" (IV).

The IV has a default value that comes with the program, and which the user can change as desired.

When the encryption process starts, the first block of the plaintext is modified by the IV using "exclusive-or" (XOR) logic. Then the encryption process begins, based on the key and this XOR process. The result is that each block of text modifies the one that follows it, and they are "chained" together. The first block of 64 bits undergoes the first of two permutations, then is enciphered 16 times, or *rounds* in eight "S boxes". It is divided into two parts and the bits are shifted around in a complicated pattern based on the key. After the 16 rounds, it undergoes the second permutation, and the next block is encrypted. The idea is that there should be no relationship between the plaintext and the ciphertext except as based on the key.

For more on the XOR process, see *How The XOR Works.*

Using the DES.

The DES itself is an algorithm, a cipher, not an actual program that you can load into your computer and use. To make it into a "user friendly" form, it is built into an *executable program*. How this is done depends on how the programmer designs it. Consequently, different DES programs use different steps or commands.

Some are menu driven, such as The Private Line; others are command line driven, such as Iris. However, no matter which way the programmer has designed it, the DES algorithm will do the encryption the same way. Assuming it is the *real* DES.

The individual steps, or commands, used might be something like this:

[01] Select the DES mode you wish to use.
[02] Enter the name of the file to be encrypted.
[03] Enter the key you wish to use.
[04] The key you have entered is [...] is this correct?
[05] Do you want to double encrypt this file?
[06] Enter the second key you wish to use.
[07] The key you have entered is [...] is this correct?
[08] Secure erase the plaintext file?
[09] Output file for data transmission?
[10] If this is correct press ENTER

[01] Remember that not all DES programs offer this choice. Some of them use only the weaker ECB mode, but you might not know that if the documentation of the program didn't tell you.

[02] With menu driven programs you can tag a file, or list of files you want to encrypt, by moving the cursor or light bar over their names and pushing the space bar. Then the program automatically finds, loads, and encrypts them. If the program is not menu driven, you have to manually type in the name and the path; i.e. where the file is located on the hard disk drive, of each file, one at a time.

[03],[06] With some DES programs the key is entered in hex, e.g. 3A-2C-FE-DF-DD-3F-2E-EF. With other DES programs the key can be plain English letters and numbers e.g. 4-N-Z-B-6-T-9-D, or something dumb, and easy for a spy to guess, like P-A-S-S-W-O-R-D. Some versions of the DES have a routine built in that will reject a key that is too easy, such as 12345678 or ABCDDCBA.

What these routines can not do is associate certain combinations of characters with the people that use them.

A dentist might think he is being clever by using a key such as I-N-C-I-S-O-R-S as it is easy for a dentist to remember.

However, if a spy knew that the person who encrypted the file was a dentist, this would be one of the first keys he would try. But the computer doesn't know that.

[04],[07] The program is asking you to verify that the key was typed in correctly and reminding you to memorize it first. If necessary, write it down, but keep it in a secure place until you have memorized it. Some ideas on this are offered in the review of MailSafe.

If you write your key on a pad of paper, the pen will leave an impression on the next page that can be easily read by tracing over it with a pencil. Tear off a single sheet and place it on a hard surface before you write it down.

[05] Double encrypting a file with two different keys will increase it's resistance to attack, depending on how it is done. More on this.

[08] Secure erase will completely eliminate the plaintext file from the disk *after* it has been encrypted. Definition of secure erase is in the glossary. Steps [04] and [07] were a hint to be absolutely sure you have the key memorized before you erase the plaintext file.

If you don't trust your memory, then write it down. If something should happen to cause you to forget the key(s) before you get around to writing them down; if you are using a high security cipher such as the DES; and you use the secure erase feature, then you have lost your data. I will mention this often: **Once it is lost, there is absolutely nothing anyone can do to recover it for you. It is gone forever.**

[09] Some DES programs have this option, used if the file you are encrypting is to be sent to another computer through the phone lines. When the file is encrypted, some of the characters that are used to replace the plaintext letters may be control characters, that could interfere with data transmission. Some communications programs will accept the encrypted file as is; some will not. Try a test message to see if your communications software requires using this option. Or maybe even read the manual.

[10] When the key is accepted and the encryption process started, a subroutine in the DES program takes the first block of 64 bits and transposes and substitutes them based on the key used; then the next, etc.

DES Programs

I have used a number of encryption programs that use the DES. Four of them are reviewed in a later section:

File Encrypt.
Iris
SuperCrypt
The Private Line

HOW SECURE ARE ENCRYPTION PROGRAMS?

This section is about attempting to break the RSA and DES ciphers; how The Datanappers might go about it, and the difficulties they might experience in their attempt. It is about a few tricks you can use to defeat them. It is also about some other types of ciphers. Some of which you might be depending on to protect your files. If so, you are about to get some bad news.

Now before one can even begin to determine how secure a particular program is, they have to know *what* it is. In researching this book I accumulated about two dozen encryption programs that were advertised as everything from "keeps honest people honest" to "unbreakable". Some of them used proprietary algorithms with names I have never heard of and have not been able to find listed in any of the many books I checked. Others simply didn't identify the algorithm used.

So what is it?

So some programs may not be quite what, at first, they seem to be. They may not offer the security that is claimed in their advertisements. But if you ask the people who produce them, they aren't likely to say anything different than what they have stated in their ads.

A catalogue I received from (someone) in the Southwest has an ad for an encryption program which "provides a high level of security for your confidential computer files".

The actual *level of security* is not stated, nor is the type of algorithm identified. Unless you can examine the source code you have no idea what it really is. And unless you are a programmer, the source is useless. In this case, it is not even available. I called the person that owns this company and hit him unexpectedly with some specific questions. This is a very effective way of getting answers. Or finding out if people do, in fact,

even have answers. Put them on the defensive.

He became quite indignant, sputtered a bit, and tried to lay a generous helping of bull on me.

"Our encryption program conforms to the highest standards..."; "it is designed to..." No numbers, no specifics, just bull. People who have a good product, know it well, and have advertised it honestly, will be able to rapid fire answers back as fast as someone asks them questions. Meanwhile, this guy will be happy to take your money and leave you with a false sense of security.

Another encryption program was listed in a surveillance catalogue I received. It offers "The ultimate protection for sensitive data", and uses another proprietary algorithm that "resists the most determined analytical attack". All this for only $395.00.

Nothing in the ad says anything about *specifically* how secure it is, or the type of algorithm used. With such a program, you don't know what you are getting, so why should you trust it? You also do not need to spend that much money to get something you *can* trust.

It Ain't Necessarily So.

Some commercial software programs have built in encryption algorithms to protect your files. While they may claim that they will keep anyone from being able to read the files they encrypt, it ain't necessarily so.

One of these is Word Perfect. The manual says "You can protect or lock your documents with a password so that no one will be able to retrieve or print the file without knowing the password; not even you". "If you forget the password, there is absolutely no way to retrieve the document." Well, perhaps not quite *absolutely*.

A program that will crack Word Perfect encrypted files is WPCRACK 1.0 - Word Perfect 5.x Password Finder.

It will, according to the author, Ron Dippold find any password up to 13 characters. On the Internet he says: "For a product such as this, it's really bad that it's so insecure. This is good for those of us who forget our passwords, but bad for someone who thinks their data is safe."

WPCRACK has been released into the public domain; it is available free. For more information on this program send Email to rdippold@cancun.qualcomm.com. (see *address* in glossary)

A Tale of Terrorists

Software Cracks Terrorists' Lock On Seized Files is the headline of an article in the 04 FEB 91 issue of Government Computer News. It tells about how a suspected terrorist group in Bolivia had a number of files that were encrypted with Word Perfect. When these files were confiscated, the Bolivian government was able to crack the password and recover the information. What they used to do this was WRPass, a password recovery program from AccessData, a software company mentioned in the next section. WRPass will recover passwords up to 23 characters long.

I tried WRPass to see for myself. Using it is quick and easy. The manual suggests that you make a backup copy and use it, rather than installing the program on your hard disk drive. To prevent unauthorized access to the program.

Since I don't have Word Perfect, one of the other computers that does was used. A text file was loaded, and encrypted with a short key. Then I popped the 5" disk in drive A

and punched in WRPass. It asked me for the access code which is printed on an adhesive label in the manual. I entered the code, and the menu screen came on.

It offers a choice of asking for more information, selecting the version of Word Perfect to be attacked, the level of analysis to be used (there are three) quitting, or continuing. I continued and was asked for the path and filename that was "locked".

This was typed in, and a bar graph appeared on the screen to show how close the process is to completion. It took about 30 seconds, and suddenly there on the screen, was the password I had used.

This is too easy, says I, and tried to make it harder for WRPass. This time a more difficult password was used, and here I encountered the only problem: finding a complicated password that Word Perfect would accept. The first one was *2$a@Z%!2b*h4b%21v*hpv2.

Word Perfect didn't like that password very much, as it refused to accept it.

A new key, *1b*jvx1$9V*6aQ29GL*4P8, which is 23 characters long.was tried. For some reason WP liked this one, and asked me to repeat it, which I did.

I saved the encrypted file, exited WP and used X-Tree to view it, to make sure it really was encrypted (it was) and then deleted and secure erased the plaintext file.

The same steps were repeated, and in about 30 seconds, there it was, exactly as it was typed in. I then went back to Word Perfect and tried the password to make sure it would work. It did.

The password feature keeps unauthorized persons from using WRPass. Another security feature in the program enables a Word Perfect user to do something that will defeat WRPass. What this is will not be revealed here, but it will not prevent the people at AccessData from breaking the password. According to the manual, they have never encountered a Word Perfect password they could not break.

This is a good product. It does exactly what it is advertised to do, and does so quickly and easily.

Programs like this are necessary, because so many people just will not take the time to memorize their passwords. They will not write them down in a secure way (more on this) and they will not use the examples included in the MailSafe manual, which will be in the coming review. So they can't remember them, and they lose their files.

With programs such as Word Perfect, lost passwords are easily recovered. With high security ciphers such as the DES, they are not. Lose your key and your data is gone forever. No one can get it back for you.

Another reason these programs are necessary. The guy in charge of the payroll department at Wexlers Widget Works discovers that he is about to be terminated. So he decides to make trouble for old man Wexler, and encrypts all of the payroll records of the employees with a different password that no one else knows. No password, no paychecks.

Indeed, there is a need for such programs, but they can also be abused. If you are going to encrypt files, do it right and use a secure program. A false sense of security is far worse than no security at all.

The files in your computer are probably as secure as they would be in an unlocked file cabinet. If The Datanappers come for them, what will you do?

What will you do?

BEWARE OF SNAKE OIL

by Philip Zimmermann.

When examining a cryptographic software package, the question always remains, why should you trust this product?

Even if you examined the source code yourself, not everyone has the cryptographic experience to judge the security. Even if you are an experienced cryptographer, subtle weaknesses in the algorithms could still elude you.

When I was in college in the early seventies, I devised what I believed was a brilliant encryption scheme. A simple pseudorandom number stream was added to the plaintext stream to create ciphertext. This would seemingly thwart any frequency analysis of the ciphertext, and would be uncrackable even to the most resourceful Government intelligence agencies. I felt so smug about my achievement. So cock-sure.

Years later, I discovered this same scheme in several introductory cryptography texts and tutorial papers. How nice. Other cryptographers had thought of the same scheme. Unfortunately, the scheme was presented as a simple homework assignment on how to use elementary cryptanalytic techniques to trivially crack it.

So much for my brilliant scheme.

From this humbling experience I learned how easy it is to fall into a false sense of security when devising an encryption algorithm. Most people don't realize how fiendishly difficult it is to devise an encryption algorithm that can withstand a prolonged and determined attack by a resourceful opponent.

Many mainstream software engineers have developed equally naive encryption schemes (often even the very same encryption scheme), and some of them have been incorporated into commercial encryption software packages

This is like selling automotive seat belts that look good and feel good, but snap open in even the slowest crash test. Depending on them may be worse than not wearing seat belts at all.

No one suspects they are bad until a real crash. Depending on weak cryptographic software may cause you to unknowingly place sensitive information at risk. You might not otherwise have done so if you had no cryptographic software at all.

Perhaps you may never even discover your data has been compromised. Sometimes commercial packages use the Federal Data Encryption Standard (DES), a good conventional algorithm recommended by the Government for commercial use (but not for classified information, oddly enough-- hmmm).

There are several "modes of operation" the DES can use, some of them better than others.

The Government specifically recommends not using the weakest simplest mode for messages, the Electronic Codebook (ECB) mode. But they do recommend the stronger and more complex Cipher Feedback (CFB) or Cipher Block Chaining (CBC) modes. Unfortunately, most of the commercial encryption packages I've looked at use ECB mode.

When I've talked to the authors of a number of these implementations, they say they've never heard of CBC or CFB modes, and didn't know anything about the weaknesses of ECB mode. The very fact that they haven't even learned enough cryptography to know these elementary concepts is not reassuring.

These same software packages often include a second faster encryption algorithm that can be used instead of the slower DES.

The author of the package often thinks his proprietary faster algorithm is as secure as the DES, but after questioning him I usually discover that it's just a variation of my own brilliant scheme from college days. Or maybe he won't even reveal how his proprietary encryption scheme works, but assures me it's a brilliant scheme and I should trust it.

I'm sure he believes that his algorithm is brilliant, but how can I know that without seeing it? In all fairness I must point out that in most cases these products do not come from companies that specialize in cryptographic technology.

There is a company called AccessData (87 East 600 South, Orem, Utah 84058, phone 1-800-658-5199) that sells a package for $185 that cracks the built-in encryption schemes used by WordPerfect, Lotus 1-2-3, MS Excel, Symphony, Quattro Pro, Paradox, and MS Word 2.0.

It doesn't simply guess passwords-- it does real cryptanalysis.

Some people buy it when they forget their password for their own files. Law enforcement agencies buy it too, so they can read files they seize.

I talked to Eric Thompson, the author, and he said his program only takes a split second to crack them, but he put in some delay loops to slow it down so it doesn't look so easy to the customer. He also told me that the password encryption feature of PKZIP files can often be easily broken, and that his law enforcement customers already have that service regularly provided to them from another vendor. [6]

In some ways, cryptography is like pharmaceuticals. Its integrity may be absolutely crucial. Bad penicillin looks the same as good penicillin. You can tell if your spreadsheet software is wrong, but how do you tell if your cryptography package is weak? The ciphertext produced by a weak encryption algorithm looks as good as ciphertext produced by a strong encryption algorithm.

There's a lot of snake oil out there. A lot of quack cures. Unlike the patent medicine hucksters of old, these software implementors usually don't even know their stuff is snake oil.

They may be good software engineers, but they usually haven't even read any of the academic literature in cryptography. But they think they can write good cryptographic software. And why not? After all, it seems intuitively easy to do so. And their software seems to work okay. Anyone who thinks they have devised an unbreakable encryption scheme either is an incredibly rare genius or is naive and inexperienced.

I remember a conversation with Brian Snow, a highly placed senior cryptographer with the NSA. He said he would never trust an encryption algorithm designed by someone who had not "earned their bones" by first spending a lot of time cracking codes. That did make a lot of sense. I observed that practically no one in the commercial world of cryptography qualified under this criterion.

"Yes", he said with a self assured smile, "And that makes our job at NSA so much easier." A chilling thought. I didn't qualify either.

The Government has peddled snake oil too. After World War II, the US sold German Enigma ciphering machines to third world governments. But they didn't tell them that the Allies cracked the Enigma code during the war, a fact that remained classified for many years.

Even today many Unix systems worldwide use the Enigma cipher for file encryption, in part because the Government has created legal obstacles against using better algorithms.

They even tried to prevent the initial publication of the RSA algorithm in 1977. And they have squashed essentially all commercial efforts to develop effective secure telephones for the general public.

The principle job of the US Government's National Security Agency is to gather intelligence, principally by covertly tapping into people's private communications (see James Bamford's book, "The Puzzle Palace"). The NSA has amassed considerable skill and resources for cracking codes.

When people can't get good cryptography to protect themselves, it makes NSA's job much easier. NSA also has the responsibility of approving and recommending encryption algorithms. Some critics charge that this is a conflict of interest, like putting the fox in charge of guarding the hen house.

NSA has been pushing a conventional encryption algorithm that they designed, and they won't tell anybody how it works because that's classified. They want others to trust it and use it. But any cryptographer can tell you that a well-designed encryption algorithm does not have to be classified to remain secure. Only the keys should need protection.

How does anyone else really know if NSA's classified algorithm is secure? It's not that hard for NSA to design an encryption algorithm that only they can crack, if no one else can review the algorithm.

Are they deliberately selling snake oil? I'm not as certain about the security of PGP as I once was about my brilliant encryption software from college. If I were, that would be a bad sign. But I'm pretty sure that PGP does not contain any glaring weaknesses.

The crypto algorithms were developed by people at high levels of civilian cryptographic academia, and have been individually subject to extensive peer review.

Source code is available to facilitate peer review of PGP and to help dispel the fears of some users. It's reasonably well researched, and has been years in the making. And I don't work for the NSA. I hope it doesn't require too large a "leap of faith" to trust the security of PGP.

How secure are encryption programs?

This isn't easy to put numbers on, as one can not accurately say that "computer X can break the ABC code in N years". There are many variables to be considered. It is usually stated as how long it would take computer X to *try all the possible key combinations* of the ABC code. The DES and the RSA ciphers can re-arrange the letters and numbers of a file in so many possible ways that they compare with the estimated number of atoms in the universe.

In the DES, the message to be encrypted is processed with a key that is 56 bits long. That's a string of 56 ones and zeros. These 56 bits can be arranged in 7.2×10^{16}th or 7.2 quadrillion different ways.

That's how many different keys there are.

"Breaking" the RSA

The process used to "break" the RSA; to find the key, to determine the primes used to create the key, is called factoring. How hard is factoring?

According to an article entitled *An Overview of Cryptography* published in LAN Times Feb. 1990, "Even with the extensive use of special-purpose hardware, 150-digit numbers would still require thousands of years to factor given present algorithms.

For several years, RSA Data Security, Inc. has offered a challenge to factor long key numbers, with cash prizes to those who are able to. They started with 100 digits and increased the length by ten digits up to 200.

The 100 digit and 110 digit numbers have been factored, but it took several months on a mainframe computer. The 120 digit one ($5,000 prize) is still unclaimed.

The keys used in MailSafe are 400 digits. PGP offers three choices; 384, 512, or 1024; and with the Iris program the user can set the length to whatever they want up to 500. Poof!

How hard is factoring?

According to the Iris help file, a computer capable of one million operations per second would require the following periods of time to cryp analyze these keylengths:

KEYLENGTH	TIME
50 BITS	3.9 HOURS
75 BITS	104 DAYS
88 BITS	1 YEAR
100 BITS	74 YRS
150 BITS	1 MILLION YRS
200 BITS	3.8 BILLION YRS
250 BITS	5.9 TRILLION YRS
300 BITS	4.9×10^{15} YRS
500 BITS	4.2×10^{25} YRS

Using keys of 200 bits can be considered unbreakable for many years to come, so if you use the RSA for the actual message encryption, you need have little concern about even the NSA breaking it. Apparently this is what the they use to protect their most secret secrets. It is also available for the public to use.

Let the feds have their secrets and let We The People have ours.

"Breaking" the DES

How hard it is to break the DES depends on several things, including the mode used (ECB or CBC) and the method of attack. More on this coming up. Meanwhile, another question asked on the Internet:

Question 1: **Is there any real, actual, documented, case of the DES having been cracked through brute force alone, in either the ECB or the CBC mode?**

All of the responses were negative; no one knew of an actual instance of this happening. However, the general consensus was that it is possible, and *probably* has been done.

*We've all assumed the spooks could do it since an article by Hellman (I think) in about 1980 showed that a parallel machine could do it.

In November 1991 I tried to sell a _____ communications system to a _____ operator in _____, and the local competition was the _____ agent in _____ who claimed to have been in a UK signals unit.

He said that GCHQ (the UK governments crypto shop) had a DES cracker which took about a week to find a key. He gave me a lot of fairly convincing details. Although this was part of his sales pitch for a non-DES encryption product, I took it seriously because he didn't appear to have the technical sophistication to have made up the details personally.

*That it's possible is accepted even by banks nowadays. See for example an article by Garon and Outerbridge in Cryptologia v XV no 3 (July 91) p177-193 'DES watch: an examination of the sufficiency of the data encryption standard for financial institution information security in the 1990's'. Their conclusion: single round DES has passed its sell-by date.

Question 2: **Is there any hard evidence that this has not happened and isn't likely to happen within n years?**

*Just the opposite, there is hard evidence that it is possible to do it even today. I have a paper here, which describes how one could build a custom mass-parallel computer, specialized in DES breaking.

The costs would be probably about 10 millions of dollars and it will probably be able to break a message by brute force in about a day. About a year ago, somebody posted a message that allegedly NSA has such machines since a long time, but they need more than a week to break a message, and they get out of order a lot.

*If you have a million chips, each needs to check 2^{35} keys; and if each checks a key a microsecond, you need 2^{15} seconds, which is under ten hours.

*Many authors focused on the 'million chips' factor and said, well, only a government or big corporation can do this kind of thing. However I pointed out in 1990 that you can trade off cost for speed. You can use ten thousand chips and get a solution in under two months, for example, and this is a construction project which an individual might be able to undertake at home.

Indeed, there are individuals that could afford to build a 1000 chip system, but for a million chip computer, probably only the federal government could build one. Or more.

Given the initial cost, and the operating cost, they would not use it for playing games. The information would have to be extremely important for them to go to such great expense, and if the sender changes keys each time, they would recover only a single message for all their trouble and your tax dollars [7]

Speculation

While most people know little about cryptography, they often have beliefs and opinions which they express. "Oh, everybody knows this, or that...) Here are a few that I have heard, along with a few comments.

One person pointed out the following article and said that the DES is no longer safe.

An article in the New York Times was headlined: *Scientists Devise Math Tool To Break a Protective Code.* The protective code referred to is the DES. The headline is a bit misleading.

Someone mentioned this article on a BBS and concluded that the DES "has been broken", but didn't mention that the article also says "Such an approach is realistic only if the codebreaker can trick his opponent into encrypting an already known message".

In other words, if the code breaker had both the plaintext and the encrypted (ciphertext) message, he would be able to compare them and derive the key that was used. Having this key, they would be able to decrypt all messages encrypted with that same key. But only that same key. [8]

Other comments:

If someone took hundreds of personal computers and programmed them to each try out some of the DES keys, they could break it.

"If an infinite number of monkeys were given an infinite number of computers, eventually they could, but they would probably write Windows 4.0 first."

The FBI could take 'a dozen Crays' and break the DES

If a large enough number of super computers were used, there is no doubt that they could. It just a matter of numbers.

A computer capable of a million DES operations per second (an operation being to try one of the possible keys) would need about 1760 years to try them all.

Such a computer may be the Y-MP C90. This is the newest Cray number cruncher, which is capable of up to 6 billion floating point operations, FLOPS, per second. Maybe so. It is a matter of translating FLOPS into DES operations, and the people at Cray won't tell me. Divide 6 billion by one million and you get 6000. That means the Cray would be able to do 6000 operations per DES operation per second. That should easily try out one key. However, this is not the way the NSA would go about trying to crack a cipher.

Question 3: **Can anyone state the amount of time a given computer would need to try out all of the DES key combinations? For example, the Cray Y-MP C-90 which is supposedly the fastest computer on Earth.**

*That's the whole point. You don't want or need one computer; it's a task that can be done in parallel very easily. A network of workstations costs much less, and can do the job just as well. See the paper cited above.

*A Cray C90 would take a very long time to do this. It just is not parallel enough. A rough estimate would be on the order of thousands of years for a brute force attack.

Custom hardware is the way to go. Currently, the limiting factor is the budget for building custom hardware. $10M would get a machine capable of doing a brute force search in a couple of hours, if not faster.

*Those are general-purpose computers. It is still not practical to use them for DES breaking. One would need a custom device, if he needs to do the breaking in any reasonable time.

*That's the wrong way to go. Do a search of back issues of Cryptologia for an article by

Richard Outerbridge on recalculating the cost of breaking DES.

*When people talk of brute force attacks on DES, a special purpose machine is assumed (i.e. 1 million DES chips, or something along those lines). Cracking DES with a general purpose computer would take an awful long time, even with a Cray or Connection Machine or whatever.

*You need on average 2^{55} tries to find a key. Remember that 2^{20} is about a million, so if you have a machine that will try 1 key per microsecond (which a Cray will do) you will need 2^{35} seconds. There are about 2^{25} (32 million) seconds in a year, so this is about 2^{10} (a thousand) years.

Now if the DIA had a thousand of these Cray's in their basement, they could reduce the time to about a year. Or perhaps two years. But consider the cost. At 30 million per, a thousand of them would set the tax-payers back 30 billion.

They would also need to build a nuclear generating plant nearby to power them.

This leaves little doubt that, as the many people on the Internet reasoned, the government has had these special machines custom built to crack codes.

Speculation:

The government has already broken the DES. They have a secret way to do it.

While no one has cited an actual case of the DES being broken, and several have stated that it is possible or probably has been done, could the DES have a secret way of cracking it; a "trap door" for example?

Question 6: **Is it possible to state for a known fact that there are no weaknesses or trap doors, or any other ways of compromising the DES?**

*Nope. No cryptosystem other than a one time pad is likely to be proven to have no weaknesses or trap doors. There is no current technology that will allow us to evaluate DES and prove that there are no weaknesses nor trapdoors.

*DES still appears quite strong, as no weaknesses or trap doors have been discovered after years of intense scrutiny by quite a few competent researchers. It is quite possible that no method of attacking DES will ever be found that is more effective than a brute force attack, however this won't prove that a weakness does not exist.

*Of course not. However, the fact that DiffCryp found that the S-boxes were better than random (rather than worse) rules out earlier fears that the non-randomness in the S-boxes were a result of NSA-inserted trap doors. There will never be such a proof.

*I can not state this, as I actually do not *know* the design-principles of parts of the DES.

*'Without question' sounds to strong for my ears. Let's say that the open research community (as opposed to MILITARY & GOVERNMENT institutions) has not been able to find a sufficient weakness which would cause DES to be considered 'broken' in the last 15 years, and that it's unprobable that there exists such a weakness. Somebody in this newsgroup even said, that DES was strengthened by it's design-principles. But I do not remember more on this topic.

*Of course not. But time has shown that DES is well designed. Other, similar, ciphers (e.g. Lucifer and FEAL) have weaknesses that DES hasn't. DES probably has weaknesses as well, but I'd still say it's the best publicly available crypto algorithm today. Please don't quote me on any of this.

*It is not possible to make any such categorical statements about algorithm strength without showing that P is different from NP, which would be a major breakthrough in computer science.

At the practical level, the development of 'differential cryptanalysis' by Biham and Shamir has shown that the design of DES was about as good as can be done for a 16-round substitution-permutation network. This has prompted Don Coppersmith of IBM, one of the original designers, to claim that IBM knew of the principles behind differential cryptanalysis when DES was designed.

*Nobody knows that. My own opinion is that there are no trapdoors, but I have no facts to back it with.

*No. But the evidence of the last few years, notably the Biham/Shamir papers, tends to indicate that DES really is strong. Shamir, who arguably knows more about DES than anyone in the civilian world but its designers, thinks that DES is about as strong as it could be, given its general design. That said, I personally believe that NSA can read DES if they want to, though at what cost I don't know.

*Nope. No cryptosystem other than a one time pad is likely to be proven to have no weaknesses or trap doors. There is no current technology that will allow us to evaluate DES and prove that there are no weaknesses nor trapdoors.

DES still appears quite strong, as no weaknesses or trap doors have been discovered after years of intense scrutiny by quite a few competent researchers. It is quite possible that no method of attacking DES will ever be found that is more effective than a brute force attack, however this won't prove that a weakness does not exist.

*No. Surely not. Chances are high that this has already happened, but did not reach my ears. Rivest(I am not sure about the name) has shown in a recent paper, that he can reduce the complexity of breaking DES by differential cryptanalysis from 56 bit keyspace to 47 bit keyspace. And I am sure, the NSA has constructed one of these machines, that contain many parallel working DES chips.

So it appears that some federal government agencies have special computers that can break the DES. The actual amount of time required, as well as the cost, is speculative, and the NSA isn't about to tell.

Double Encryption

How does double encryption work, and how secure is it?

One way is to encrypt the file twice, using two different passwords. Now one might logically think that this would double the equivalent key size (usually called key*space*) from 56 bits (7.2 x 10 ^16) to 112 bits (5.19 x 10^33).

One person who claims "many years of experience" told me that this method of double encryption can raise the keyspace to the equivalent of 2 ^ 57. While this is a definite increase in protection (where 2 ^ 56 is 7.2 x 10 ^16th, and 2 ^57 is 1.44 x 10 ^ 17th) it is far from doubling the effective keyspace.

A better way is to first encrypt the file with one key (A); then decrypt it with the second, different key (B), and then encrypt it again the third time with the first key (A). You will see the expression A,B,A in coming sections. This is what it means.

Back to the Internet...

Question 5: Does double encryption, meaning encrypt with key A, decrypt with key B then encrypt again with key A, actually increase the resistance to attack? Can anyone put numbers on this?

*Since DES has been shown to not be a group, this would in fact increase the security. It effectively doubles the length of the key, so a brute force attack is out of the question for the time being.

*The effective strength of this method is likely less than 112 bits, as differential cryptanalysis may very well be effective in this case. Differential cryptanalysis is the method of attack that was shown to make keys longer than 56 bits no more secure than 56 bit keys for DES.

*This is now the way DES is used by IBM etc. It is thought to be completely resistant to all known attacks.

*Most people think that it is indeed stronger.

*Yes. It's widely agreed, that this would correspond to a DES using a keyspace of 112 bits. Somebody with more theoretical knowledge - please back me up.

*Yes, it does. It wouldn't, if DES were a group, i.e. if a double encryption were equivalent to a single encryption with a different key. But it has been recently proven that DES is not a group, therefore multiple DES encryption does increase the security.

*Yes. DES has been shown not to be a group. Therefore, this doubles the key length, greatly increasing the security. Even better is triple encryption, in CBC mode, with separate IVs for each of the 3 stages. The effective key then is 360 bits.

Triple encryption? A 360 bit key? Poof. A 360 bit key makes for 2.35 x10 ^ 108 different key combinations.

The Cray C-90 that can do a million DES operations per second would take something like 7.4 x 10 ^68 trillion trillion centuries to crack such a keyspace encrypted message. Such long keys are ridiculous. The Earth will have decayed in its orbit and fallen into the Sun long before then. Poof!

There is another way of increasing the security of the DES that works automatically, and doesn't require typing in the keys three times.

The Whitening of the Keys

Whitening, actually pre-whitening and post-whitening is a process used by MailSafe. When it uses the DES key, it does some tricky things that makes the effective keyspace 120 bits instead of 56. This is something like using two different IV's or two more encryption steps, and makes the data appear more random, and therefore much harder to attack.

The actual mechanics of the process are a little complicated and not really important here, but it achieves this increased security without changing the DES into something that no longer is the DES. At 120 bits, the Cray mentioned above would require about 421 million trillion centuries to try all the keys. Or something like that. Poof!

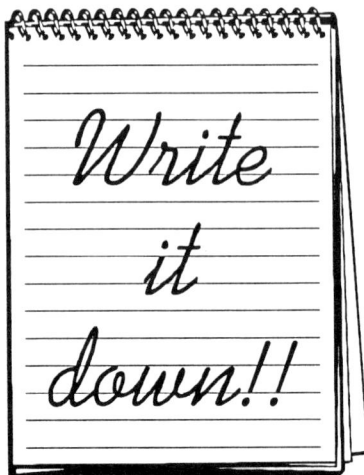

If you can't remember keys very well, use a made up nonsense phrase that isn't easy to forget, but write it down first.

Keep it in a secure location, and remember to tear off the top sheet before you write. The pen leaves an impression on the next page which can be easily recovered.

THE KEY TO THE KEYS

The weakest link in the encryption security chain is not usually the cipher, it is keeping track of the keys. Not only does there have to be a way to keep the wrong people from getting them, there has to be some way to keep the right people from *for*getting them. For an individual who has only one file they keep encrypted, there is only one key to remember. Or two, if they use double encryption. One or two keys shouldn't be that hard to remember, right? Perhaps.

If a person has dozens of files they keep encrypted, they have a decision to make. If the same key is used for all of them, and that key is compromised, then someone can decrypt all of the files. If a different key is used for each file, then there is the problem of remembering all of them, as well as which key goes with which file. Trying to remember a lot of different keys is not a great idea.

One can compromise by placing the files in groups, with each in a different subdirectory, each with its own different key. This reduces the risk and make it easier to keep track of the keys. Having them in groups also simplifies copying them to floppy disks; each subdirectory can be limited to what will fit on a floppy disk. Dolphin Encrypt is a useful program here, as it will encrypt an entire floppy disk (or hard disk subdirectory) in one operation.

> *File Encrypt is, overall, one of the fastest encryption programs. You can go to the subdirectory where it is kept, and start encrypting a file within a few seconds.*

Another situation is where a number of different people use the same computer, and each person has a different set of files that they are allowed access to. This is a good application of the Local Encryption feature of MailSafe.

Many people can use the same copy of Mailsafe on the same machine. Each has their own login name and password, and can have their own personal subdirectory containing the files they are allowed access to. Since each user has their own password, they can access only the files encrypted with that password. [9]

The Iris disk has a utility called Merlin that will automatically encrypt all of the files in a subdirectory.

What it actually does is copy the files to a floppy or another subdirectory, and DES encrypt them as they are being copied. The secure erase feature can be used to eliminate the plaintext.

OK, by spreading a large number of files over several subdirectories, with a different key for each, there is less risk and fewer keys to keep track of. However, even with just a few keys, you still need a way to keep them secure, and unless you can absolutely trust your memory, you need a way to keep a record of them, that no one can get to. Ultimately this comes down to one simple thing: You have to remember *something*.

Your Own Secret Code

Here is a simple little substitution trick you can use to keep encryption keys, or any small amount of information, secret. For those of you who have no trouble remembering such things, no problem, you don't need this, but many people do. That's one reason for software companies like AccessData, remember?

Bob might have trouble remembering numbers. He has to write down Alice's unlisted phone number, but he doesn't want to keep it in his wallet, or anywhere his wife might find it.

The new payroll supervisor at Wexlers Widget Works might not be able to remember the password to the computer program that is used to make out the employees paychecks, so where can he write it down that no one else can find it? The employees at Wexlers seem to be having a hell of a time getting paid...

No matter how good or bad our memories, all of us have something so burned into our synapses that we will never ever forget it. Like the phone number of our first love back in the second grade. Think about it.

These few digits can be added to, or subtracted from, a password, another phone number or teller machine code, to make something that can safely be written down. *As long as it is something that can not be traced back to you.*

You use the number 1947263 as a password. Your sandbox sweetheart's phone number was 954-1632. Add them together and you get 11488885. If necessary, when you write this new number down, add a note such as what her name was. Alice, what else...

A simple little trick that could keep forgetful people from losing their data, and it has an interesting side effect. After you have used it a few times, you discover that you no longer need it. For some reason you end up memorizing the keys. Funny how that works, but it does.

Try it and see for yourself.

Pocket Databases & Racehorses

A useful device for storing keys is one of those credit card size data banks that store names, phone numbers, and the like. Some of them are password protected, so no one is able to get to your secret keys. right? Well, maybe.

I read a story about a guy who was making book, who used one. He got busted, as bookies sometimes do. This bookmaker had a lot of secrets in his little database, but he wasn't worried. He used a password. Right.

The police took it to the manufacturer, who was able to defeat the password protection and get all his secrets.

The bookie got six months, and rumor has it that the cops made a bundle on the third race at Bay Meadows.

Should you use one of these for storing your keys, remember two things: They can be defeated, and they can also lose their memory, and your keys, if the battery is removed. Another good idea for easy to remember passwords is in the review of MailSafe.

Any of these little tricks help in keeping your keys and passwords in a secure way in case you forget them.

Whatever works for you...

At this point in Digital Privacy, you have a good idea of how secure encryption programs are, and how to keep your keys safe. In a coming section will be reviews of a number of programs, which may offer some ideas on deciding which one you might want to use, but first let's consider how much security you need based on who might want the information you have. And what they might do to get it.

SO WHO CARES?

Who would want the information in your computer? Who would spend the money and take the risk involved in stealing it? Or trying to steal it.

For the federal government to want the information you have, it would probably have to concern "National Security", some sort of crime, drug dealing or perhaps mass software pirating, or have to do with a political organization that the administration doesn't like. Like in COINTELPRO where the FBI burglarized the offices of the Socialist Workers Party something like 60 times.

If a business, a big corporation, were to want your files, they would have to contain information that is valuable to them. They might try to steal a formula or new widget design that would be useful, but otherwise why would they bother? If you have none of this kind of information, you have little to worry about from big business or Big Brother. If you do, consider the next section.

Espionage!

Now and then on the TV news, we hear about so and so company getting caught spying on some other company. Big deal. Same old spy story. By the time the late movie comes on it is forgotten. Most people don't remember the story because it is of no personal interest to them. They also don't know that these infrequent stories are the tip of the proverbial iceberg. You might find the chapter *"Who's (bugging) Who?"* in *The Bug Book* interesting.

Most instances of spying are never revealed. For many reasons. Would you tell the world if someone had successfully bugged your office or broken in and stolen a computer file?

You also don't often hear about bribery and extortion and blackmail. These are tools of the espionage trade. Just like a lathe or a screwdriver, they are something to be used when the situation calls for them. A big corporation that would find a "legal loophole" and use it to cheat their employees out of their pensions, or that would deliberately subject them to dangerous working conditions, would hardly hesitate to set up and blackmail a computer operator of a competing company. The wouldn't hesitate to break in, or sneak in, to get the files they want. Where millions of dollars are at stake, life becomes very very cheap.

Someone Cares

So, let us assume that you do have something that someone else wants. Something they were willing to spend time and money to get. Here are some ideas on how they might go about it.

First they might consider whether or not they want you to know they are spying on you. If they think that you will continue to receive or generate useful information, they will probably keep their actions secret as long as possible.

If conditions are right, they might use van Eck monitoring equipment. While this may not get them the actual files they want, they might at least get the names of the files, and the subdirectories where they are stored. They might even get the keys used to encrypt them. Some ideas on making your system secure against van Eck snooping will be in a coming section.

Another possibility is to tap your phone line. If you are sending any of the wanted information to someone else, they will be able to intercept it.

Otherwise they might just break into your home or office and make copies of the files they want. There is much you can do to make this difficult for them.

Confusing the Datanappers

If you are like most computer owners, you will have accumulated a large number of floppy disks. Perhaps hundreds of them. If you were to place the backup disks that have sensitive encrypted information in a large box with all of these other disks, it would make them harder to single out.

Assuming, of course, that you label them right. It wouldn't be the brightest of ideas to write "Secret files I am hiding from the FBI" on the label.

Consider something like "SHOOT-MUP.GAM" or "XXRATED.GIF". Then encrypt the files on a bunch of other disks that are no longer useful. Your backup copies of old games you don't play any more, the hundreds of shareware files you downloaded and never use, or whatever else you can find.

If The Datanappers do break in they won't know which disks they want; they won't likely have time to make copies of all of them, and they probably won't take the whole box as this would tip you off.

But even if they did take or copy all of these disks, cracking them would be an almost impossible task. If they have a special DES machine that can break a single encrypted file in 24 hours, and you have 100 disks with 10 files on each one, it would take about 3 years to crack all of them.

What could be so important that they would do this?

The Spooks in the Cellar

Now, in spite of all your precautions, The Datanappers have managed to get copies of these files. They take them to an underground room at Ft. Meade or the computer lab at their corporate headquarters, and start to analyze them. How to they do this? Just as one has to know what a cipher is to determine how secure it is, one also needs to know what it is to break it. So they first thing to do is try to figure out the cipher that was used.

Theoretically, any good cipher will produce ciphertext that looks like random bits to anyone who doesn't have the key. In reality, though, some ciphers have identifying patterns or unencrypted characters that reveal them.

A file encrypted with MailSafe in the local utilities mode has the letters H ENRSAF at the end of the file, and if it is encrypted for transmission and has a digital signature, it includes the name of the recipient and their public key.

The PGP program has BEGIN PGP MESSAGE at the beginning and END PGP MESSAGE at the end, and Dolphin Encrypt 1.72 has the numbers 9876543210 at the beginning of the encrypted file. Other encryption packages, such as the DES produce no identifying information in the ciphertext; it looks like purely random bits.

I used the X-Tree view feature to look at several other encrypted files. The Vernam has no identifying plaintext, but the Playfair cipher would be easy to identify because it converts the encrypted file into only the first 128 ASCII characters. So it should be easy enough for the spooks to narrow it down.

Now as to the method of attack, if a public key system is used, they probably won't try to derive the key through factoring; because keys over 400, which MailSafe uses, or 512 which is one of the three choices in PGP, just can't be factored yet. So they will attack the actual message, or perhaps try Trickery to get the key. More on this.

If they narrow it down to PGP, which means they are up against the IDEA cipher, or if they determine that MailSafe was used, I suspect they would go to plan B which is Trickery. With the pre and post whitening, it's not possible to break. Not yet. As of this writing, I did not have any information on how the IDEA cipher might be attacked.

If they believed any of a number of proprietary ciphers was used, they no doubt have programs designed to attack them.

Now suppose they are convinced the cipher used is the DES. If they are agents of the DIA, then one must assume they have one (or more) of these special made machines consisting of a million, or whatever, DES chips. Other agencies may or may not have such machines. Little doubt that the CIA does, and the FBI probably does, but other government agencies may or may not. If not, they may be able to convince those agencies who do that your disks are worth their time to crack.

If such a computer can, in fact, crack the DES in a matter of hours, it would be faster to use this *brute force* method than to try Trickery. More on this.

So they begin. If the message were single encrypted, then they would probably be able to break it within hours, or perhaps a few days at most. If they can't crack it in the amount of time it should take, then they will know that something has been done to defeat this brute force attempt.

It might be double encrypted, or an unknown cipher might have been used.

If they have reason to believe that the message has been double encrypted, then they presumably won't be able to break it with brute force, so they might try *Dictionaries*, or something I call *Trickery*. Both may involve DFO. Such methods would apply also to other ciphers, including unknown ciphers,

or a combination of ciphers as is used in SuperCrypt and Encrypt-It for Windows.

Attack!

The term *attack*, or *cryptanalysis*, means to try to break a cipher, and there are various methods that can be used.

Some of these are ciphertext only, known plaintext, chosen plaintext, and differential cryptanalysis.

In ciphertext only, one attempts to break the cipher, or derive the key used, by statistics, frequency of characters, and having an idea what the encrypted message says. If it is a technical manual, or is in a particular language (German, Spanish, etc).

Known plaintext means looking for particular words or phrases; any strings of characters the codebreaker would recognize.

Chosen plaintext is based on *plaintext ciphertext pairs*; having both the plaintext and ciphertext to work with. If the codebreaker has both, it is possible to compare them and find the key. Possible, but not easy.

Differential Cryptanalysis is a complex attack based in part on analyzing the ciphertext, making changes in it, and analyzing it again to see the result of these changes.

Trickery

Trickery is a method of attempting to crack an encrypted file by guessing what key might have been used. DFO, Dumb Foolish Operator, is a term for people who use their license plate number for a key, and don't use secure erase.

Dictionaries

People often use common ordinary words as keys; words that can be found in a dictionary. Intelligence agencies know this, and they have programs that will feed in and try all of the words in a dictionary. They might have different levels they would try; they might start with Websters New World and work up to the complete Oxford Dictionary of the English language. Perhaps depending on the level of education of the person who encrypted the file.

> *If The Datanappers believed that double encryption were used, they might apply special programs that would try a word, take the result, and try a second word, then try the first word again. The result of each of these attempts would be scanned for recognizable combinations of letters. To try all of the dictionary words this way could take a very long time, but it probably can be done.*

What might be easier is a custom dictionary. Trickery. A custom dictionary would be a list of possible keys based on what they know, or can find out, about the person that encrypted the file.

Every day, more and more records are being digitized and stored in massive data banks which can be accessed by different government and private agencies. Filed under the subjects SSA number, they will eventually contain every record the person creates during their lifetime.

Any name you have ever used, every address and phone number you have ever had, the license plate and VIN numbers of every motor vehicle you have ever owned, bank account numbers, serial numbers of firearms you own or used to own, library card, insurance policy, and drivers license numbers, details on every job you ever had, and any other numbers they can tie to you. These are all things people might use as passwords.

Successful intelligence consists of, among other things, obtaining every last scrap of available information. No matter how obscure it seems, each is one part of the puzzle.

They might also use the same numbers as they apply to people you know, live with, are related to, work with, etc. It is not beyond the realm of possibility that someone might use their next door neighbor's telephone number for a key. *Who would ever think of that?*

I suspect that agencies such as the NSA also have enormous libraries of words that they can customize into special purpose dictionaries. By entering a series of key search phrases, they could select probable words to use from any number of categories.

Suppose you are an EE who graduated from Ohio State. They could do a search for words and phrases that relate to both OSU and engineering. Names of the buildings on campus, the instructors, the streets on and around the campus; electrical terms, names of people who invented electronic equipment, and the like.

> *People who are smart enough to use encryption programs are not necessarily smart enough to use keys made of random characters or obscure phrases.*

All of these possible keys, and all of the different ways the letters and digits that make them up could be arranged would be tried. If they were determined enough, they might also throw in anything that is even remotely associated with anything in your life. If they should learn that you sometimes consult an astrologer, they could plug in a dictionary of astrological terms. If they find out you were a caddie one summer during your high school years, they may use a dictionary of golfing terms.

If this seems like a lot of different things to try, consider that, at most, they might come up with a few thousand terms or names or numbers for a given individual. Just for the sake of argument, say they came up with ten thousand. Or a hundred thousand. A fast mainframe computer or mass parallel DES chip system could try all of these in a few hours. Brute force against a DES double encrypted file just is not feasable.

RUPA and The Average Bell

We have seen some huge numbers here, how many thousands of years, or centuries, computer X would require to try all the keys of the ABC cipher. But they wouldn't necessarily have to try all of them. The right key will not necessarily be the last one tried. This is one of the factors mentioned above, where I said that how long it takes to "break" a code depends on a number of things.

Just before I dropped out of Economics 105, the instructor in a RUPA lecture hall was rambling on about bell curves and averages and other exciting stuff. If a cryptographer were to encrypt, and then decrypt, an infinite number of messages, he would find the right key, on average, about half way through the total number of possibilities.

Meanwhile, as the monster computers are crunching away at your secret files, they obviously have to have a way of knowing when they have found the right key.

Boilerplate

As each of these possible keys are tried, the computer looks at the result, searching for something it can recognize.

Each group of 8 binary bits (ones and zeros) equals one ASCII character; one out of a total of 256. ($2^8 = 256$) Some of these 256 are the letters A to Z, the digits 0 to 9,

and punctuation marks. The rest of them are special graphics and control characters. The computer will be looking for the ASCII characters that are letters and numbers and also some of the control characters, such as tabs and carriage returns. This might identify the word processor used to type the files, which may help the process a little, because of the way they are placed within a document.

Several small groups of characters, each followed by a carriage return, could be the beginning of a letter. They might look here for a date, the city and state, "Dear ..." and like that. At the end of the document they would look for such strings as "Sincerely", and "Very truly yours". This is called "boilerplate" and is one of the easier parts of a document to decrypt because the cryptographers have a good idea what to look for.

If you were to delete these strings, it would make the message harder to crack. If that isn't feasable, then you can "pad" the beginning and end of the message with random, meaningless characters. If you have information that could still be important many years in the future, little tricks like this can be used.

With more and more documents being sent by electronic mail, more and more documents are being intercepted. They can be labeled with the date and names of the sender and recipient, and stored away for when it becomes feasable to break them. Government spy agencies realize that this can happen, which is one reason they use such very high levels of security in encryption and communications. Most individuals do not realize this, which is why they don't.

Data Compression

Another way to confuse The Datanappers is to compress a file before it is encrypted. Compression is a method of squeezing a file into a smaller size. Being smaller helps increases its resistance to attack; there is less to work with. Some programs, MailSafe and PGP, have this feature. Some others do not, but you can use any compression utility, such as PK-ZIP.

Having learned about the different ciphers available, it is time to decide which one, if any, you want to use. That's what the next section is all about.

There is nothing wrong with using an encryption program that provides more security than you really need, but if using such a program requires manually typing in dozens of file-names, it becomes very time consuming and expensive.

WHICH PROGRAM IS RIGHT FOR ME?

It seems (so far) that the only available ciphers that are secure against attack by the Spooks in the Cellar are the RSA, the DES, & IDEA . Other ciphers, the Playfair, the Enigma, etc, can not be counted on for high security. A new program, Dolphin Encrypt which was just received, is reviewed here.

The RSA, with a long key, is unbreakable at present, as is the double encrypted (A-B-A) DES.

The IDEA cipher has resisted attack for several years, but it is still relatively new, and has not withstood the test of time as has the DES. Earlier, you read what the experts had to say about the possibility of the DES having a secret way of breaking it. All of them agreed that there is no way to categorically state that there is not. The same applies to the IDEA cipher.

At this point it becomes more a matter of your particular application; how you will use the cipher, how often, how many files are to be encrypted, how many people have access to the computer, and etc. In the reviews coming up, you can learn the details of a number of programs, and then decide.

DOS, Macintosh or Unix?

All of the programs reviewed here run on DOS computers. PGP can be modified to run on a Unix computer, and File Encrypt runs on both DOS and OS-2

A number of security programs are available for the Macintosh and the Amiga, but I have not tried them as I don't have either of these computers. Novatronics produces a program called Directory Opus that encrypts files for the Amiga, and this computer will also run some DOS programs with the installation of a hardware device.

Compact PRO is an archiving program for the Mac which has an encryption feature, FileGuard and Mac Password are access control programs, and Cassidy & Greene produce a system called Access Managed Environment which, I am told, is an excellent multi-user access control system.

RSA Data Security is working on an end user public key program for the Macintosh and other operating environments, including Unix. No release date has been announced, but according to the company president it is "well under development".

For building encryption into commercial programs, RSA Data Security produces BSAFE which is a developers toolkit. It provides encryption of local files, E-Mail, and other features, and can be built into any software application. It is already being used in Lotus Notes, the Apple System 7 OCE, and many other products and systems by Motorola, DEC, IBM, Novell, Sun Microsystems, Xerox, and others.

RSAREF and RIPEM

RSAREF (RSA Reference) is a tool-kit; a library of programs written in C and provided in source, which can be used to "facilitate rapid deployment of Internet Privacy-Enhanced Mail (PEM) implementations.". It is source code that can be used to write a complete public key electronic mail program and not a ready to run program. If you are not a C programmer, it won't be of any use to you.

RSAREF is distributed free by RSA Data Security, Inc through the Internet. For details on how to obtain RSAREF, send E-Mail to rsaref-administrator@rsa.com or write to:

RSA Laboratories
Attn: RSAREF Administrator

101 Marine Parkway Ste. 500
Redwood City, CA. 94065

RIPEM is a public key PEM electronic mail program that uses the RSA and DES ciphers, similar to MailSafe (but it is not MailSafe). It was written by Mark Riordan, based on RSAREF.

RIPEM is available to users in the US and Canada, on the Internet, and includes a license from RSADS for non commercial use.

RIPEM is provided in executable form, and will run on DOS, Mac, and some Unix machines, such as SunOS, NeXT, Linux, AIX, and ULTRIX. It also includes the source code.

RSA Data Security, Inc. is now including RIPEM with RSAREF.

The MailSafe main menu. The right & left cursor (arrow) keys are used to select which of the five sub-menus you wish to use.

Then just follow the prompts (instructions) to prepare a message for E-Mail transmission or "local" encryption.

MailSafe is the only menu driven public key program available.

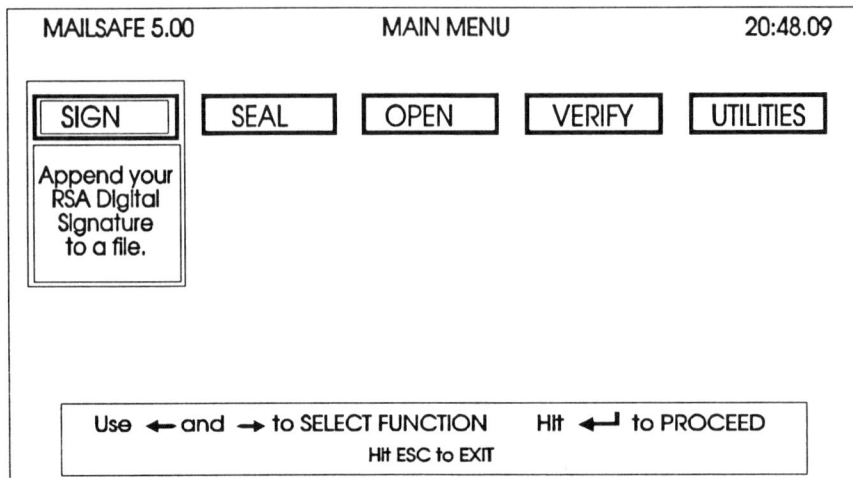

```
 ┌──────────────────────────────────────────────────────────────────┐
 │  MAILSAFE 5.00              MAIN MENU              20:48.09         │
 │                                                                    │
 │  ┌─────────┐   ┌────────┐  ┌────────┐  ┌────────┐  ┌──────────┐    │
 │  │  SIGN   │   │  SEAL  │  │  OPEN  │  │ VERIFY │  │ UTILITIES│    │
 │  ├─────────┤   └────────┘  └────────┘  └────────┘  └──────────┘    │
 │  │Append your                                                      │
 │  │RSA Digital                                                      │
 │  │Signature                                                        │
 │  │to a file.                                                       │
 │  └─────────┘                                                       │
 │                                                                    │
 │     ┌────────────────────────────────────────────────────────┐    │
 │     │ Use ← and → to SELECT FUNCTION   Hit ↵ to PROCEED       │    │
 │     │              Hit ESC to EXIT                            │    │
 │     └────────────────────────────────────────────────────────┘    │
 └──────────────────────────────────────────────────────────────────┘
```

SOME PROGRAMS REVIEWED

This section is a review of encryption programs, based on having personally used them. They are in alphabetical order.

Dolphin Encrypt

There are two versions of Dolphin. Ver 1.72 is the "bare bones" release and ver 2.10 is the full featured, "advanced" release.

Ver. 1 is small, only 59K, and for a command line driven program is as easy to use as one could want. To encrypt a file enter DE E filename, and then when prompted, the key (10 characters minimum) to be used. The program first runs a virus self check, which takes only a few seconds, and then the process begins. A bar graph appears at the bottom of the screen to let you know how far it has progressed, and when completed, it advises that the encryption was successful and the amount of time it took.

Decryption is just as easy. Type in DE D filename, and the key.

Ver. 1 also offers the choice of encrypting "in place" (the actual file is encrypted) or making an encrypted copy, leaving the plaintext file unchanged.

The Advanced version of Dolphin has an optional function that no other cipher has. You can encrypt files using a code phrase following the password and if it ever becomes necessary, because of a lost or forgotten key, Dolphin Software can recover the key for you. However, this feature is included in the program only if the user specifically asks for it. Otherwise it will not be on the disk. Although some people won't much like the idea that their encryption program can be broken, others may like knowing that if an employee, like the payroll manager at Wexler's, changes keys to prevent anyone from accessing the company

files, they can recover it. Other features of Dolphin are the ability to encrypt an entire floppy disk, (both DD & HD); it supports a script language for writing complex commands; a multiple file text reader; file comparison; file purge (secure erase); and four different bar graph programs for analyzing-frequency and distribution of characters.

How secure is Dolphin Encrypt? From the manual: Dolphin Encrypt uses several different kinds of pseudo-random number generators (all tested to ensure that they produce acceptably random numbers), and multiple versions of some of them. These are used at different stages during the encryption, in computationally complex ways.

The block size used in encryption is not constant. Random bytes are added at various stages. The input key is converted into a longer key which is itself modified and encrypted (in a way that depends on itself) multiple times during the encryption process. The encryption and decryption of any particular byte in the plaintext or in the ciphertext depends not only on the key but on the values of preceding bytes in the plaintext. This is a process carefully designed to remove all discernible order from the plaintext.

Dolphin Encrypt allows the key to be up to 60 characters in length (the key must consist of at least 10 characters) and there are 68 possible characters which can be used. Thus the number of possible keys is the sum of the number of possible 10 character keys, plus the number of possible 11 character keys, and so on... This sum is approximately 9×10^{109}.

The new Thinking Machines super computer, capable of a trillion operations per second would require more than 10^{90}

years to break the Dolphin cipher using brute force.

The Advanced version is even more secure than ver 1.72 so the two are not compatible.

Encrypt-It for Windows

As Digital Privacy was almost complete, I stumbled across Encrypt-It on a BBS called The Rising Storm. It was incorrectly labeled as a collection of True-Type fonts, which, like all people in Desktop Publishing I obsessively collect.

Reading the document file, I learned that this program was written to run under Microsoft Windows. EI does not include a 'setup' or 'install' file, so I loaded it from Program Manager. It installed quickly, and with no problems, and has a nifty little icon of a safe with the letters "DES".

The opening screen has a dialog box which offers you a choice of registering, information about shareware, the benefits of registering, and using the program.

The main screen has the usual Windows menu and the file list box, which makes it very easy to call up the files to be encrypted. Files. It does batch encryption, which is a very nice feature. Just click on the *'select all'* box to tag all the files in that subdirectory. A user shouldn't have to type in a long list of filenames to encrypt them.

However, when I started to encrypt a file, I noticed that the DES is not included in the shareware program. This was a demo only, and not the full featured program. To get the complete program, you have to send in the required fee. Since the DES is not included, and the cipher that is used is not identified, I decided not to do the speed test. [10]

EI has some interesting features; one is a bar graph that shows the frequency of use of all 256 ASCII characters in a file, and another is "military grade" secure erase.

What this does is delete the record of the file from the FAT and then overwrite it nine times. First it writes a series of 0-1-0-1-0-1... then reverses it and writes 1-0-1-0-1-0... and then the Hex character F6. This is repeated twice.

Secure erasing this way will, according to the author, eliminate any possibility of the information ever being recovered.

Unfortunately, there wasn't time to get a registered copy to complete the review, but based on the demo, this is a very nice program. It is easy to use, and has nice features.

There is something interesting that I noticed in the documentation file:

We use multiple layers of encryption, with DES as the final layer of protection for your data. Because of this approach, we feel your data is protected far better than using DES by itself. Following that was: *Encrypt-It implements a version of Vernhams machine developed at Bell labs in the 1920's as part of its lite encryption method.*

File Encrypt DES

I first heard of File Encrypt in an article in Byte Magazine (June 89) called "Secret Codes". The article was written by the same person who wrote the program, Mr. Asael Dror of Wisdom Software in San Francisco.

File Encrypt is a bare bones implementation of the DES. It is a very small file, (35K) written in assembly language and will run on both DOS and OS2 systems.

It is not menu driven, does not have the compliance test, choice of DES modes (apparently it uses the ECB mode) or any of the features that some other implementations have.

To start the program, go to the subdirectory where it is and type "fe", or you can add it to your path statement and run it from anywhere on the drive.

File Encrypt will then ask if you want to encrypt or decrypt; the name of the file (it will find it in any other subdirectory); the key to be used; and whether or not to secure erase the plaintext file *after* it has been successfully encrypted.

File Encrypt is the *overall* fastest and easiest to use of all the programs reviewed here. Even though TPL and MailSafe do the actual encryption a little faster, with FE you can open the program from the command line, and have the encryption started in a few seconds.

The Iris DES

The DES program that comes with Iris disk (version 4.1) allows the user to select which of the DES modes they want to use, it has secure erase, the DES compliance test and it will output encrypted files for modem transfer.

Version 4.1 is not menu driven, so requires entering the instructions from the Iris command line. (I spoke with Mr. Moreton some time ago, and he said that a menu driven version was being developed. I have not seen it available yet.)

To encrypt a file the you type the following:

Iris command cipher /function = encrypt /algorithm = DES /mode = CBC /keyvalue = abcdefgh /input = filename /output = filename.

At first, particularly for someone not used to working from the command line, this seems confusing. It takes a while to get used to it, but after you have used it a few times it becomes easier.

Iris has a very good help file that can be used on-line. Just type 'help', and then select the

subject you need help with. You can also print it on paper, or to a file.

A number of other files are included on the Iris disk. One is *Merlin* which is a batch encryption utility. Merlin will encrypt all the files in a subdirectory automatically, using any of the ciphers on the disk.

The others include the Playfair, Littlewood, Bazeries, and Vigenere ciphers.

The Iris Public Key Program

The public key program on the Iris disk is, like the Iris DES, a bit tricky to use. To encrypt a file, first you generate a pair of keys as described above. Then to encrypt you type in: Iris command cipher /function = encrypt /algorithm = RSA /keyname = unity2 /input = mysecret /output = mysecret.cpr

Unity2 is the name of the public key to be used, 'mysecret' is the file to be encrypted, and 'mysecret.cpr' is the name of the file after it has been encrypted.

Use it a few times, and make a few notes, and it becomes easier, but this is still a long command to have to type in if you have a lot of files to encrypt. However, one can write a batch file, and also use Merlin for multiple files.

Now the difference between Iris and PGP or MailSafe is that it uses the RSA for the actual message encryption. While this means it doesn't run as fast as the others, it makes encrypted files more secure than any other program available to We The People. Apparently it is this method of encryption that is used by the DIA. With a key of 400, it isn't likely to ever be broken. Poof.

While Iris does have a message authentication feature, the present version lacks a sophisticated and easy to use key management system. These are supposed to be included in a future release.

Note: I just spoke with Mr. Moreton, who advises that he is not going to produce a new version of Iris. In the next month or so, he is going to release the Iris source code into the public domain.

The MailSafe Public Key Program

Where the PGP and Iris public key programs can be copied from the floppy disk they came on to a subdirectory and then used, MailSafe has to be installed.

This is a simple process that takes just a few minutes. If you don't know how to use DOS commands, the 127 page User Reference manual shows how to do everything that is required, one step at a time.

The first step is to create two subdirectories and copy four files to them. You can also modify the path statement in your auto-exec.bat file if you like. This enables you to run the program from anywhere on the disk; you don't have to switch to the MailSafe subdirectory.

Then type 'MailSafe' to open the program.

Now you need to generate the two keys. Type 'genkey' and follow the prompts. This is a one time operation. According to the manual, "This can take as long as 15 minutes, but is usually only 2 or 3." It is the fastest of the three public key systems; on my 386 it took nine seconds.

Next, you are asked to enter two names. First, a short 'login name' such as your first name; then an 'official name' such as your first and last names or first initial and last name. The login name is usually kept short; 8 characters or less and the official name can be up to 78 characters.

Now the program asks for a password, which can also be up to 78 characters. It does not echo (appear) on the screen as you type it in. Very useful feature in case enemy agents have a van Eck van parked across the street.

With a 78 character length available, it is safe to use only letters, and not a hard to remember string that includes digits and punctuation marks.

Nonsense phrases make good passwords as they are easy to remember and something no one else would think of.

"When I was one old little boy I lived behind a purple meadow" is something made up, and would not be found in dictionaries. It would be virtually impossible for anyone to think of this same exact phrase. It has 48 characters that can be arranged in any of 8.3×10^{67} ways.

Another example, from the MailSafe manual, is to use an acronym: Creamy Red Yellow Pickles Taste Outlandish; CRYPTO.

The last thing you are asked for is the zone you are in. Since one of the choices was not Twilight (which is what it's often like around here) I entered Pacific standard. This is used to add (stamp) the time and date to a message you send. This completes the installation, and now you are ready to use MailSafe.

From the command line, type in 'MailSafe' (or run it from Windows) enter your user ID and password, and the main menu pops on the screen. There are five options as shown in the computer generated drawing.

SIGN, SEAL, OPEN, and VERIFY were explained earlier in this chapter, which you can refer to.

The UTILITIES menu has five choices: Local, DOS Utilities, Public Keys, Special, and Config.

DOS Utilities has commands for managing files without having to leave the MailSafe program. You can call up any subdirectory on the disk, and Copy, Rename, Move, or Delete files.

Public Keys is where you can Certify other people's keys, List certificates, Delete expired certificates, etc.

Special is for computing, viewing, and comparing Message Digests.

Config(ure) is used to configure MailSafe to your system, to turn off and on some of the MailSafe features, set, or change, the time zone, turn the computers speaker off and on, and etc.

The last selection, **Local**, may be the most useful of all for some users.

The name MailSafe may imply that it is a program made only for encrypting messages that are to be sent to others. Actually MailSafe can be used to encrypt any files that are on your hard disk drive, whether you will ever send them through electronic mail or not.

You may have noticed that I make a big deal of menu driven programs and batch file encryption.

Why should I have to type in all the file names from the command line? That's what computer programs are for; to do the work for me.

MailSafe's local encryption feature does this for me.

To use it, select the Utilities menu and follow the prompts. You can select any subdirectory on the disk, and pick any file to encrypt, or you can use the tab key to tag all of the files in that subdirectory. Then hit enter, and MailSafe automatically encrypts all of them. This speeds up the overall process considerably; a subdirectory of 56 files, totaling 178K, was encrypted in 69 seconds. Very useful when enemy agents come beating on the door in the middle of the night.

One warning: MailSafe encrypts the actual file, not a copy. There is no plaintext file left. While this eliminates the need for secure erase, remember that if you forget your password, your files are forever gone. There is no way to recover them.

MailSafe Command Line

Command Line is a program that works in conjunction with MailSafe, so that it can be accessed and run from the DOS command line, or from within another application. Included with Command Line are source code routines that can be used to "port" MailSafe into, for example, a communications program.

If you have spies in the field who need to send encrypted information from portable computers through unsecured channels (the phone lines or cellular radio) they can call up MailSafe from their communications program, encrypt the information, and send it in without having to leave the program.

The PGP Public Key Program

The PGP public key system, written by Philip Zimmermann, is a free program which uses the IDEA cipher for the actual message encryption and the RSA to encrypt the IDEA key.

The IDEA cipher is believed to be very secure; expert cryptographers haven't been able to crack it yet. However, it is fairly new.

PGP2.1 does not have graphics menus like MailSafe, SC and TPL, which means it isn't as easy to use. However, it isn't as difficult as Iris.

When you start the program you get an information screen that explains how to generate a key, and encrypt a file, and some other features. The generate a pair of keys, enter "pgp -k" from the command line and follow the instructions. First it offers a choice of three key lengths, 384, 512, or 1024 (poof!) bits. You decide which one you want, and then type a string of random characters. Then it starts the calculations. A

512 bit key took 75 seconds to generate on this 386.

The program then asks you for a user ID, and a separate passphrase (this can be as long as you want to make it) which is required to access and use the keys. You have to type in this password twice to make sure you got it right, and it does not appear on the screen.

The command to encrypt a file is: pgp -e filename username.

If the file is 'mysecret', and the person I am encrypting the file for is Linda, then the command would be [pgp -e mysecret Linda]. The program would then encrypt the file using Linda's public key.

To decrypt a file sent to me, if the filename was 'goodies' and my public key were 'semispy' I would type in [pgp -d goodies semispy]

While PGP is fast, it does not allow for multiple file encryption. I tried this using different subdirectories and wildcards, and files in the same subdirectory as the program, but it wouldn't work. To be fair, it should be added that PGP is intended for encrypting E-mail, and not local encryption.

The more advanced features of PGP, such as key management, are just a bit more difficult to learn. You need to spend a little time and perhaps make some notes to really understand it. This is made much easier by reading the excellent documentation files.

The Private Line DES

The Private Line (ver 7.04, Sept 1990) is a true DES encryption program produced by Everett Enterprises. It is menu driven, very easy to use, fast (it is written in assembly language) and has *almost* all of the features one could want from a DES based encryption program. You can:

*Select which mode is to be used; ECB, CFB, or CBC
*Enter the key in either hex or plain English.
*Double encrypt. (This is not the A,B,A method)
*View files in hex.
*Create subdirectories without having to leave the program.
*Output the file for modem transmission.
*Run the DES compliance test.

To use TPL, copy the files from the program disk to whatever subdirectory you want, and then type "private".

TPL begins by running the DES compliance test, which takes a few seconds, and then the main menu appears. You are offered a number of choices; the ones listed above and others from a second menu. Here you can make changes to the secure erase feature, create directories, turn the computer speaker off or on, etc.

To encrypt a file, you select the subdirectory, tag the file, and begin encrypting. TPL is that quick and easy to use. Just follow the menu prompts and you can be up and using the program five minutes after you get it. Should you need it, there is a detailed manual included on the disk.

A new Windows version of TPL is to be released sometime (no release date announced) in the future. This will include the one feature that I would like to see: the ability to tag a list of files and have TPL automatically encrypt them and secure erase the plaintext files.

SuperCrypt DES

The copy of SuperCrypt I used is the shareware demo version, which I downloaded a long time ago from some BBS or other.

The first thing I noticed about SC was the opening screen reminding the user that it is not public domain, and that they should send in the registration fee. OK, not unusual.

A second reminder is that you have to hit the $ key to start the program. Then there are two more screens, again asking that you send them the registration fee.

Then the program opens.

While you are in the program (but not while a file is being encrypted) it interrupts you with a beep and yet another reminder to send them money, and in order to exit the program, you are hit with two more screens, asking that you send in the registration fee.

Sheesh. Ain't exactly what I call subtle. However, these many reminders are removed from the registered version.

SuperCrypt has nicely designed screens and handy pull down menus, and it is very easy to use. To encrypt a file, just pull down the encrypt menu, and follow the prompts.

When the file list screen comes on, it lists the files in the same subdirectory where SC is, but you can quickly change to any subdirectory you want. You can also tag one or more (up to 1000!) files and SC will automatically encrypt them. Very nice.

With each file is a notation of how long SC will take to encrypt that file, in either of two modes. Long as in very long. See the speed test below. SuperCrypt would be a very nice, user friendly program if it weren't so maddeningly slow.

About these two modes. One is another proprietary cipher, and the other is the DES. Quoted from one of the help screens:

Supercrypt provides a very secure, multiple method, approach for encryption & decryption. It also provides tools to help you analyze the encrypted code. and also: *If you choose the DES level of encryption, your files are first encrypted /decrypted using several traditional encryption methods, then processed with the very secure DES.*

Elsewhere in the help files it says that SC "implements a version of *Vernhams* machine" (which, you may remember is an XOR process) but doesn't identify the rest of the "several traditional encryption methods".

Sound familiar? You might have noticed that in both SuperCrypt and Encrypt-It, *Vernam* is spelled *Vernham.* Hmmm.

A few days before Digital Privacy went to the printer I got to thinking about this coincidence, the spelling of Vernam, and the other similarities between SuperCrypt and Encrypt It for Windows, so I called the author of EI, David Black.

Interesting coincidence, I mentioned, and also that SC is distributed in Texas, EI in Oregon, and he lives in Colorado.

"Oh, I wrote SuperCrypt" he told me, and explained that he used different distributors for the two programs. SC is still available, but has been replaced by Encrypt-It for DOS. Or as he put it, "EI for DOS is the second generation of SC". It has some new features, and is also much faster, he added. It is also compatible with EI for Windows; encrypt with one, decrypt with the other.

I asked about EI; if it has a choice of DES modes, and other things. No, but a new version is coming out in March that will use the CBC mode, and will have some other goodies.

An increase in speed, along with batch encryption makes for a nice encryption program; the only one I know of that is a Windows application.

Mr. Black also told me that a "very security conscious manufacturing company in Florida" uses EI, and that he has sold a 5000 user site license to "a large organization" neither of which he identified. Apparently they trust it.

Shakedown

All of the programs reviewed here were put through a series of tests. A large number of files, exe and com, text, and graphics, were encrypted and double encrypted, encrypted with a different program and decrypted, compressed and uncompressed, copied back and forth from one logical drive to another, renamed and named back, and then decrypted. All of them worked perfectly. Not a single problem.

The DES Compatibility test

One implementation of the DES should be compatible with another. If you encrypt a file with one DES program, you should be able to decrypt it with a different DES program, assuming, of course, that the same key and mode are used, and that the initialization vector in the CBC mode is the same.

"The IRIS implementation of DES is faithful to the NBS specification, and should be compatible with any other DES implementation. IRIS has been checked for compatibility with one other software DES implementation known as 'The Private Line' and was found to be compatible in all modes." Mr. Peter Moreton, producer of IRIS.

My findings are the same as Mr. Moreton. A number of files were encrypted with each of the four programs and I tried to decrypt them with each of the others. The files encrypted with Iris were successfully decrypted with The Private Line, and vice versa. Neither Supercrypt or File Encrypt would do this. In all tests the same file, and the same key was used. It was tried in all available modes. SuperCrypt uses other ciphers with the DES, so I didn't expect it to work, but File Encrypt should have.

The Speed Test

To compare the speed of these programs, a 379K text file was encrypted and timed as it ran. TPL was fastest at 32 seconds, MailSafe 40, PGP 50, FE 53, Dolphin 82, and SC 577 seconds.

The Iris programs were not timed as the disk was somehow damaged and there was no time to replace it.

Running under Windows

All of these programs, except PGP, will run from Windows as non Windows applications. PGP doesn't want to work from Program Manager, but you can switch to DOS and run it.

Cost

DOLPHIN I,	$64.00
DOLPHIN II	$128.00
PGP	FREE
TPL	$30.00
FILE ENCRYPT	$69.95
IRIS	$39.00
MAILSAFE	$125.00 *
SUPERCRYPT	$49.00
ENCRYPT-IT	$59.00

* I just learned from RSADS that MailSafe is now available for $50.00.

Encrypting Graphics Files.

There is nothing in the doc files of these programs about encrypting graphics files. It shouldn't make any difference, but they were tested just to see for sure.

Files 4 and 5 in the speed test were a vector and a bitmap file. Both were encrypted and then decrypted, and then imported into Corel Draw!. They were all reconstructed without any problems. This may be useful information for spies that want to hide stolen blueprints. Also for pirates and their treasure maps.

System requirements

All of the above programs run under DOS, and will work on a dual floppy disk drive system, though a hard disk is recommended. They will run on a PC, XT, AT, 386 or 486 with 640K or more RAM. Public key programs have to crunch some very large numbers to generate the keys. While this is a one time thing, it can take some time. Depending on the system and the key length, this can be from a few seconds for a 486 or fast 386 to several hours for an XT. If used on a slower machine, one can let it run overnight.

No Guarantees.

The information on encryption programs presented here is based on having used them, the doc files, and other sources of information including the Internet newsgroups. While I can not personally guarantee that any of these programs do not have a secret way of breaking them, it should be pointed out that the people who provided answers to my questions are scientists, software engineers, university professors, and cryptology experts. I believe the information here is accurate.

Recommendations

None, really; it is up to the individual to decide for themselves. As far as my personal choice, I have practically every encryption program available to the general public, and can use which ever one I want. I use Mail-Safe. There are several reasons why. With MailSafe I can keep a large number of files encrypted, in groups each with a different key, and still have only one password to remember. MailSafe is a public key program, so I can also use it to send E-mail. It is menu driven, fast, easy to use, and costs only fifty bucks.

Encryption and the law

While there are government agencies that don't much like the idea that We The People can use encryption programs that they can not break, there are no laws that specifically prohibit this. None of the lawyers I asked knew of such laws. This could change.

As you may recall from the introduction, SB 266 would have forced software manufacturers to provide the government with a way to break into any type of encryption algorithm used in their programs. Another, similar, bill will come along sooner or later. Such champions of tyranny as Senators Biden and De-Concini never give up. They'll be back.

But by then, We The People, having been forewarned, will have had plenty of time to obtain secure programs.

When people fear surveillance, whether it exists or not; when they grow afraid to speak their minds and hearts freely to their government or anyone else, then we shall cease to be a free society. Senator Sam J. Ervin.

PART II: THEFT AND PREVENTION

Keeping your confidential files encrypted is the single most important thing you can do to insure your Digital Privacy.

This will keep The Datanappers from being able to read your files, but even so, it is a good idea to do whatever you can to keep them from being able to make copies of these files. Sometimes you forget to encrypt one, or you are in a hurry and put off secure erasing the plaintext of something you did encrypt.

There are also people who might steal your computer. This might be because they want the information that is in it, to keep and use, or to sell. This part of Digital Privacy is about restricting access to your computer, and securing it against theft.

If you have confidential information that concerns others on your hard disk drive, you also have a responsibility to these people to make sure it stays confidential. This is a something you should not take lightly. In England, there are laws that require this, but in America, apparently there are not. I talked to several attorneys that specialize in computer law, and they told me that they knew of no law that specifically dealt with the confidentiality of files *because they are in a computer.*

If I could access the computers in 100 different doctors and lawyers offices, I suspect that I could easily copy files from every single one of them. I also suspect that maybe one or two of them might use data encryption. Maybe.

A few years ago, I bought a used Seagate ST-225 hard disk at a garage sale in Los Gatos, California. I installed it in my old 286 and discovered that there was information still on it.

The drive's former home was a doctor's office, a specialist, who kept information about his patients on the drive that now belonged to me. Personal and medical information. Names and addresses and diagnoses, credit card numbers and unlisted phone numbers. All kinds of confidential information about his patients. If you live in the Silicon Valley area, you might have been one of them. All this information was in files that had been "erased" but which were easily recovered.

The drive was reformatted to destroy this information, but there are people who might have used it to their own advantage.

Alarms and locks

If an experienced burglar wants to get into a place to steal data, or a computer, there is a very good chance that they will be able to. Because it is often so easy to do. Depending... Some government agencies, big corporations and large office buildings have very good security measures to help prevent this. They have guards stationed at the doors and wandering through the area 24 hours a day, TV cameras, high security locks, and all that. This can make it very difficult (though not by any means impossible) for a spy to get in.

Fine for them, but what about a persons home, or the offices of a small company? They often can not afford such security measures, which places them at a higher risk. A few things to think about:

Burglar alarms may or may not be useful, with emphasis on not. In any large urban area they will probably be ignored for hours. In a residential area they are more likely to attract attention, but only because the noise of the ringing bell bothers the neighbors. When someone finally gets around to checking out the situation, the thief can have gotten in and out and gone. In a rural area where the nearest house is a mile away, they are completely useless.

Alarms also aren't much use if they can be defeated, and virtually all of them can be.

An alarm system that is set up with a company that will send security guards around to see what is happening is better, but this too, can take some time, and an experienced thief will cut the phone line which will defeat most of them.

Closed circuit TV systems are useful only if there is someone watching the monitors; someone that will investigate if they see anyone prowling around. It does little more than add insult to injury to watch a videotape of someone copying your files. Someone you will never see again, because they were flown in from a thousand miles away for this job, and were probably disguised anyway.

Many people in the security business agree that secure locks are more effective against burglars than are alarm systems. What most people don't know is the difference between a low and a very high security lock.

Some years ago I enrolled in a correspondence school (The Belsaw Institute) to learn locksmithing. When I got my "Official Locksmithing Student ID Card" I ran out to get a set of picks. To practice on, I bought a brand of padlock that you have heard of. This was the first time I had ever used picks, and I had it open in ten minutes.

My front door took quite a bit longer (and also attracted a fair amount of attention from the neighbors) but I got it open. Another brand name that you would recognize, and which I replaced the next day.

While manually picking a lock can be successful, something that is much faster is an electric pick. Used by someone who knows how, most, but not all, locks can be quickly

opened. Many of them within a few seconds. The odds are that this includes the one on your front door. ...**within a few seconds...**

I have personally tried out these devices. They really do work, and they are available to anyone who is determined to get one. Think about it...

Very high security locks, such as Medeco and Abloy, can be installed, but even they are useless if the windows are easy to open.

The best way to keep your computer, or your data, from being stolen is to make the area too hard for thieves to get into. More often than not, if they see that it is secure, they will look for someplace that is easier. As one can tell from the numbers of burglaries reported by the media, it is obvious that there are a lot of them. [11]

Gadgets and Gimmicks

There are ways to defeat secure locks and other perimeter defenses. Some high security locks can be drilled, and if they can't, the door itself probably can. A hydraulic jack can be rigged up as a "spreader" that will force a doorjamb open. There are many more such tricks. If someone tries to break in, here are three ways you can know about it before they succeed, and do whatever is necessary to stop them.

The Sensaphone Security System, available from Global Computer Supply, can be set up in the area where the computer(s) are and if it "hears" loud noises, such as someone trying to break down the front door, an alarm bell, or even a smoke detector, it will dial up to four phone numbers, repeatedly, until someone answers. Then a synthesized voice will tell whoever has answered what the problem is. Such as you, or a neighbor, or an answering machine...

Another nice feature it has: you can call it to check in. The same electronic voice will report the time, temperature (useful for large systems in temperature controlled rooms) and then activate a microphone, just like an infinity transmitter, so the caller can hear what, if anything, is going on.

Sensaphone can be used with a number of other detection sensors including visible light and infrared. It has a battery backup for power failures, and plugs into a modular phone jack. The base price is under $250. I haven't tried Sensaphone, but it looks like a decent deal to me. It's about the same price as the infinity transmitters that will be featured in *Sources*, but with lots of extra features. The one weakness is the phone line. If it is cut, Sensaphone won't phone.

If one of the employees of the company you work for lives a short distance away, you can use an alarm transmitter. It can be set to start transmitting its signal if something is moved or opened or whatever. Magnetic or pressure sensitive switches on the outside doors will activate it if they are forced open.

Such a system, with a **possible** range of ten miles, depending on conditions, can be set up for less than $200. As it is not drawing any power when it is not transmitting, it can be battery operated, and since it doesn't depend on the phone line, there is no way to defeat it from outside. For more on this see The Bug Book.

In the beginning of this section I said that closed circuit TV cameras aren't much good unless someone is watching.

Executive Protection Products, Inc. of Napa, California sells (or leases) a system with which you can monitor your office through the phone lines. The system consists of a video camera and transmitter , and a monitor used at the receiving end. It will work with up to five cameras, and sends a still frame "snapshot" every 12 seconds. The complete system sells for about the same price as a high end 486 computer system.

Boobytraps, Booby Hatches, Barristers.

Another method of preventing computer theft is to booby trap the area. Done the right way, it can reduce significantly the chance of legal problems, and still be a deterrent.

Legal problems? Indeed. In my last year of college, someone tried to break into the electronics lab. While crawling around on the roof, the hapless thief lost his footing, fell through a skylight, and was cut by the broken glass.

It wasn't hard to find him, as the police responded to the alarm in time to track him by following a trail of blood.

Well, he was arrested, but later he filed a lawsuit against the college. Seems they were negligent in not making the roof safe for burglars or some such thing. Sheesh.

I graduated before the thing was settled, so I don't know how it turned out, but in this perverse system of "justice" we have, he might well have won a substantial sum of money.

So if you have thought of some clever tricks to, uh, "discourage" a potential thief, make sure they don't backfire on you.

A flashing strobe light concealed behind a louvered air vent can have a disorienting effect on a burglar in a dark room. Remember disco? Very loud noise can add to the confusion, such as a sound effects tape of sirens or dogs barking, or maybe the 1812 Overture at 105 decibels. A burglar can't be expected to work under such conditions, so they will probably split and look for someplace easier.

Any electronics technician can set this up, as well as the alarm transmitter.

An Inside Job

All your valiant efforts have failed, and a burglar has managed to get inside. All is not lost, as there are a few things that can help prevent him from making off with your shiny new BelchFire 486 with the CD ROM drive. And some that may not.

Global sells an anti theft device called Cablelock that will chain a computer to something too big and heavy to easily move, like a desk. Similar to the way writers are chained to their desks.

Cablelock uses "technologically advanced adhesive compounds" a fancy name for glue. Polymers, epoxy, semantics. Glue.

The one pictured in their catalogue is mounted to a PC case. Which is painted with enamel. A hammer and screwdriver will take the thing off in two seconds. Maybe not separate the *advanced adhesive compounds* from the enamel, but it will rip the paint off the case, and the damage will be so slight as to not ruin the resale value. This product offers better security for the monitor, as they are made of plastic. To remove the plate would probably ruin the case, and the resale value.

What most people apparently don't realize about burglars, especially ones that specialize in computers, is that they are much like Boy Scouts; prepared.

PC Guardian Security Products, in San Rafael, California, makes something a little better. They have cable locking devices that are mechanically mounted to the computer case and monitor. How this is done depends on the system, but they can be used without drilling holes or anything that would void the warranty or effect the resale value.

One of these devices, for the PS/2, uses a bracket that is bolted to the back of the case, and then secured with a steel cover and a padlock. The way it is installed there is no way to remove it without damaging the case.

What's to prevent someone from cutting the cable? Nothing. If they brought something to cut it with. These are not intended as the ultimate anti-theft devices, they are made to prevent casual theft; to stop someone from walking off with a computer in a retail store or office. Actually, they do more than this; if the thief plans on selling what he steals, he's less likely to take it if he can't do so without damaging it. *Even if he cuts the cable, he still has to get the lock off.*

PC Guardian is the manufacturer of these products, and they sell direct to the end user. Most of them are under a hundred bucks.

Doss Industries makes a sheet metal locking system for computers. It consists of a base plate that is secured to the surface it sits on (desk, workbench, etc) with *an adhesive substance*. A second plate is mounted to the computer and secured to the base plate with a lock.

Glue. I suspected that this was something that could be easily pried loose, so I called the manufacturer.

Not likely, they told me. They tried it with a tire iron and were not able to remove the base plate. They also told me that no one has ever reported to them that a computer, secured with this device, was stolen.

This product also has holes in the base plate so it can be bolted to a desk or table. If you ever do need to remove it, there is a way. This information is included in the instructions. It does so without causing damage to the surface it is mounted on. Its one weakness is if it is applied to a surface that has old chipped paint on it, which could be torn loose.

A number of computer retailers were surveyed to see if they sell any kind of anti-theft products. Not even one. Someone at one of these stores said "We'd rather sell them another computer". While this is not implied to be the attitude of all computer retailers, it is interesting that none of them sell such devices.

If you have a computer in a tower case, there is an easy way to secure it. Most of them come with a metal (some are plastic, if so they can be replaced) base plate that is mounted to the bottom of the case with sheet metal screws. The base plate could be easily bolted to the floor using wood screws or lead anchors. The slots in the screws could be filed down, or you can use special screws made with one edge of the slots already cut away. They can be tightened but not loosened.

The case would be ruined, and also the resale value, if someone tried to rip it loose, and drilling out the screws may take too much time and make too much noise.

Access Control

Another important area of Digital Privacy is controlling who has access to your computer. Who as in someone who might break in, and also those who have access to the area; employees who have keys, night shift workers, maintenance personnel, and of course the cleaning lady who is secretly a CIA operative. Operative. Rumor is they don't use the term *agent*. Here are a few ideas.

The Stacker Attacker Defeater

If you use Stacker, then you already have a very effective access control system that you probably didn't know about.

Stacker is a data compression program that reduces the size of the files on a hard disk drive. It compresses them, and when you want to run a program, it uncompresses them back to normal size so you can use them. This nearly doubles the capacity of the drive; a 100 Mb drive using Stacker can hold about 175 Mb of files.

When you start up your computer, the operating system reads two files called *autoexec.bat* and *config.sys*. The information in these files does a number of things, one of which is cause the Stacker program to run. The data, being compressed, can't be read by the operating system until it is uncompressed, and if the operating system doesn't see these two files, it doesn't get uncompressed. So to use this as an access control system you can:

1. Set your computer BIOS to boot from the A drive.

2. Format TWO floppy disks with system, and copy the autoexec.bat and config.sys to these floppies.

3. Delete the autoexec.bat, config.sys, command.com and io.sys files from the hard drive.

Now the computer will not boot without one of the floppy disks.

If someone should try to start up the system, they will see the error message on the screen, and may realize *part* of what you have done. So if they should have a boot disk with them, or bring one next time, the computer will boot. However, all they will see is that Stacker is installed, and will not be able to access any of your files. As far as the computer is concerned, they don't even exist.

Only if they can duplicate the information in your autoexec.bat and config.sys files, can they access your data. An experienced operator *might* be able to do this but it would take time. Perhaps hours. A clever idea that you can use for free.

Why TWO disks? The other is a backup.

Data Security Plus!, also from PC Guardian, is a software package that provides any combination of six functions. You can select the ones you want, without having to pay for the ones you don't. The six modules are:

1. Access Control.

With Access Control, you can set up the computer with password protection for 10 users on three levels. There can be 8 general users, 1 local administrator, and one corporate administrator. It also has a one time use password feature for the general users, should they forget theirs. But, as we have learned so far, no one ever forgets their password, do they? If more than a certain number of incorrect passwords are entered, the system gets cranky and shuts down.

The other five are:

*Program approval (only approved programs can be used) and virus control;

*Directory locking; restricts access to subdirectories;

*Audit trail, which keeps a record of users, logon attempts, programs used, and time and date;

*Data encryption; a proprietary cipher;

*Forced backup. This is another clever idea. It forces the user to make backup copies every so often. Something a lot of people need to be reminded of...

Data Security Plus appears to be easy to use, based on the well written 166 page manual that comes with it, and while it works with compression programs such as Stacker, it does so only if the C drive is not compressed. Since drive C on this computer is compressed, I wasn't able to review it.

Most IBM clone computers have a lock on them. What it usually does is disable the keyboard.

While working for a computer company assembling systems for customers, I learned that the keys that were supplied with most systems were all the same, just like handcuffs. Later, when I bought my old 286, the salesman handed me the keys and said something about security.

I said that I already had a key, as they were all the same. He denied this (maybe he really believed it) so I took the one that was on my key ring and went around the store turning the demo models off and on. Made him very unhappy, but he has a responsibility to his customers; he should have known better. He does now. So don't count on the lock that came with the computer to keep anyone out of your system.

An Ace lock switch (Ace brand made by the Chicago Lock Company, the kind used in vending machines) is available from any locksmith shop for about fifteen bucks and can be installed in a few minutes.

This won't prevent someone from removing the case and connecting a jumper across the switch terminals, but it keeps honest people honest. A better idea is to install a second switch that turns off the power to the hard disk drive. Then mount a *secure* padlock to the case so they can not open it. While it is possible to drill out the bolts that hold the latch in place, again this makes noise and takes time, and ruins the resale value.

Something that will prevent anyone from using your system is the Personal Access Security Board, also available from Global. This is a circuit board that plugs into a slot on your computer motherboard.

Once installed, your computer will not boot until you enter the password, even if a boot disk is placed in drive A. It has an "on line lock" which allows you to leave it running and no one can access it while you run out to pick up a pizza. It also has a "password history" feature that keeps a record of any attempts made to use the system. Works on the XT, AT, 386 and 486.

At a little over a hundred bucks it ain't a bad deal, and for a few bucks more, you can get one that has a motion detector. If the computer is moved, it goes off and makes a lot of noise. This is one of those things they you will forget about until you decide to rearrange your desk.

A few more products from PC Guardian: First, they have a lock that fits over the power switch so no one can turn the computer on. With desktop computers, the switch is usually inside the power supply, so it can't be defeated by opening the case and jumping the switch.

Next there is a similar device that is installed on the back of the computer. It covers the plug to the keyboard, and has a switch that goes in the cable to turn the keyboard off. You can't swap keyboards because the plug is blocked by the locking steel shield. This could be defeated by cutting the keyboard cable and splicing the wires together, but otherwise no one can use the system.

Also available from PC Guardian are "Floppy Drive Locks". These clever little gimmicks fit into the slot in the drive and are held in place with an Ace lock. These, too, are made of steel, and can't be removed without damaging the drive, and it can still be used when they are in place. If you are working on something that is sensitive, you can make backup copies without removing the locks. Nifty idea.

Data To Go

All of these ideas and products will help prevent anyone from getting in, and accessing or stealing, your system but

suppose all of them should fail. This isn't likely, but just in case, there is one last thing that will absolutely positively prevent them from stealing your files.

Recently, a new product called the Floptical Disk Drive hit the market. Floptical means, of course, *floppy optical*, and is a drive that holds a 20 Mb optical disk. It will also read from and write to, regular floppy disks. Fascinating! With one of these nifty drives, you can copy 20Mb of confidential information to a disk you can carry in your shirt pocket. Then you can **secure** erase it from the hard disk drive if you are going to be away from your system for an extended period of time.

Another way to "take it with you" are the Portable Hard Drive from Liberty Systems. These disk drives are 2 x 5 x 7 inches, have capacity of 40 to 425 Megabytes, and plug into the parallel port of any DOS computer, including portables. If you have only one parallel port, you can plug the printer into the drive; daisy chain it.

So how do you access it? When you buy one of these drives, you get a software package that does all this. At the end of the day, you can take all your secrets home with you.

You might remember back in March 1971 someone broke into the FBI office in Media, Pennsylvania. Whoever it was took a number of files that were later published by an organization called WIN.

Well, it's a good thing for the FBI that they didn't have a computer with a hard disk drive, or they might have lost a lot more files.

Today all FBI offices have computers. Lots of them. So they don't take the chance that this could happen. According to the people at Liberty, the FBI and the Secret Service use their drives.

So can you.

The Datanappers can't steal what isn't there.

Portable Computers

Many people are toting portable computers around nowadays. Sometimes they have valuable, confidential data on them, which creates considerable risk; they are very easy to steal. Or leave in a cab or hotel room.

There's not much that can be done to keep people from forgetting them, but there are a number of things one can do to make them harder to steal, and also harder to access the data if they are stolen. Finally there are a few things one can do that might get their computer back if it is lost or stolen.

The Notebook Guardian from PC Guardian is a plastic coated steel cable with a loop at one end and a lock at the other. The lock mounts to the side of the computer the same way as desktop computers; they are mechanically installed rather than glued on.

As well as securing the computer to the cable, it also locks the computer closed. You can't open it without removing the lock. If the lock is forcibly removed it can break the case and destroy the resale value.

They are available for Mac, Compaq, NEC, Toshiba, AT&T, Dell, and IBM, and others. Under $100.00. Call for details.

Kensington Microware offers a similar product, called the MicroSaver, which has the lock mounted through a slot cut into the side of the case. Like the Notebook Guardian, a broken case ruins the resale value, but if a spy is interested in the data, rather than the computer, then breaking the case is not important.

While the loss of a portable is a considerable expense, sometimes the data on its hard drive is even more valuable. Trade secrets, formulas, or the game plan in a big money civil suit. How important is the data to someone else?

The Security Group offers an engraved plate that is glued to the bottom of your portable. It has a registration number and an 800 number for a database called STOP, which maintains records of systems reported stolen. This information is available to law enforcement agencies. Registration and the plate costs $25, which is a small price to pay for even a slight possibility of getting your computer back. While a thief can remove the plate, this will leave a "scar" that will make reselling it more difficult.

PC Guardian sells a theft recovery service called *COP*; Computer Owner Protection, made by IDX Technologies. It works with both desktop and portable computers.

COP is a program that generates an identifying number which is hidden in the computers root directory. When you install it, this number, and your name and phone number, are copied to the program disk, which is then returned to IDX.

Should the computer be stolen and later recovered, the police can type in C:\COP and the owners name and identifying number appear on the screen, along with the message "STOLEN COMPUTER". You can add this to the path in your autoexec.bat file so the computer starts beeping, and the same message flashes on the screen whenever it is booted up.

A neat idea. It might just get you your computer back, but it could have an interesting side effect. You are half asleep at 26 thousand feet, and suddenly remember that you didn't get a report finished. So you pull out your portable, set it on the little fold down tray, and fire it up. The guy in the seat next to you, who just happens to be an FBI agent, sees STOLEN COMPUTER flash on the screen. It would be interesting to hear you explaining it to him. I wonder if they issue some kind of wallet size plastic card with the computers serial number on it, just in case...

Another thing you can do is use a soldering iron to engrave a phone number and the offer of a reward for its return on the bottom of your portable. This might well be as effective as the above services, and it doesn't cost anything, but as they are so inexpensive, why not do both?

The LapGuard from Personal Computer Card Corp is another interesting product. It requires that a special disk with a code number to be placed in the floppy drive to use it.

No disk, no DOS. Won't get it back if it is stolen, but will slow down The Datanappers. And you, too, should you lose the disk.

Secure Technologies makes a gizmo called Lap Secure. This is a small plastic device that has to be placed in front of a sensor mounted to the side (inside) of the computer to turn it on. Interesting idea.

Of the many products listed in this book, there is one in particular that I think is special. For a number of reasons.

This is the model SL007 portable computer from BCC in the California Silicon Valley. It uses the Intel 386SL microprocessor, has a 64K cache memory, and runs at 25 MHz. A fast portable. Actually, they call it a "notebook". Semantics.

The Double-Oh-Seven encrypts data going to and from the hard disk or floppy drive, using the DES. The *real* DES. With a choice

of modes. Load a file and it is automatically encrypted. Try to use or view the file, and it asks you for the key. If you don't have the key, you don't get to see the data.

The encryption process is done with the VM007 DES chip, made by VLSI; apparently the same one used in the custom made computers the government uses. As far as I know, this is the only portable that has the DES built in.

The SL 007 is a very nice little computer. It is built into a nicely shaped "Soft-Touch" case which is esthetically pleasing.

A few of the many features of the SL007 are:

*It comes with an 80 MB hard disk drive, and a 120 MB drive is available as an option.

*It comes with 4 MB of RAM, and can be expanded to 8 MB.

*It has a Hi-res VGA (640 by 480) display with 32 gray shades.

*It has a battery life of 2 to 3 hours in the DES mode, 4 to 6 in non DES, and recharges in 1 hour.

*It has a built in FAX and 2400 baud data modem.

*Would you believe that BCC actually has a toll free number for tech support? They do. Are you listening Bill Gates?

In addition to all this, I would like to point out something quoted from their brochure: [The SL 007 is] *"Designed, Engineered, and Manufactured in the USA. "* If you have read any of my other books, you might recall that I have said (more than once) that there is absolutely nothing wrong with buying American made products.

Compare this little gem with other portables that have similar features, and you'll see that the price of the 007 ($3500.00 street price) is not all that unreasonable. Add to that the

DES security it provides and you have a most attractive package. If you are considering buying a portable, I hope you will give the SL007 the consideration it deserves.

The single most important, and the cheapest and easiest, way to keep your private files private is to encrypt them.

If computers continue to increase in speed as they have in the past, in a few hundred years it may be possible to factor a 400 bit RSA key. If we continue to trash our Earth as we have in the past, there won't be any life left by then.

PART III: THE INVASION OF THE DATANAPPERS

Practically everything you do creates a record. Write a check, use your American Express or ATM card, enroll in a school, visit a shrink, buy a car or a gun, get a fishing license, fly somewhere on an airplane; do any of these things and you leave a record behind. Filed away in government and credit reporting agency computer files, these records create a profile which reveal a great deal about your personal life, and can be used for many purposes.

Not so many years ago, there were no computers capable of processing and storing such massive amounts of information.

But with the technology of today, such mass storage exists. Something like five pages of information about every person in America can be stored, and quickly accessed, on a single computer. Eventually every one of these records will be massed in one centralized location.

For now, this is an almost impossible task, but as computers continue to get cheaper and faster, it becomes more of a reality. Something that may make this even easier is the subject of the next section.

NEURAL NETWORKING COMPUTERS

The "Neural Networking" computer is a fairly new development based on an idea formulated back in the 1950's; how memory, (RAM or Random Access Memory) in a computer is accessed, and a better way to do it.

Computer memory is composed of individual bytes, each of which can store one character, and has its own individual address, much like the houses on a street. One RAM chip holds a certain number of bytes, just like one block has so many houses.

When a byte of information is to be sent to memory, the microprocessor consults something called the program counter, to get the next address that is to be used. This is like a supervisor telling a mail carrier which house to deliver a letter to, except that the computer generally gets it to the right address where the US Postal Service may or may not.

Well, in our analogy, the people who live in these memory houses are not very friendly. They don't know their neighbors, and never communicate directly with them. Like in some big cities. So it is with RAM. One byte has no knowledge of what is stored in the others, or that other bytes even exist, and the microprocessor doesn't know what is in each byte address until it reads it.

Consider the task of writing a letter on a word processor.

As each character is typed on the keyboard, the microprocessor sends it out to the addresses, one byte at a time. When the letter is done, the program retrieves all this data, again, one byte at a time, and sends it to the printer.

Now supposing that all of these memory houses were connected together. The people in them could communicate directly with each other. They could call each other on the phone or meet at the back fence, drink beer, burn steaks and compare information.

Neural networking works something like this. It is based on the way the brain (the biological type) does things. As it says in the article quoted below, the human brain has a hundred billion neurons (writers slightly less) each of which are connected to thousands of others.

From Neuron Digest, 09 JAN 92 Vol. 9, Issue 1:

Basic neuroscience research has produced abundant evidence that the nervous system is a complex organ that cannot be viewed simply as a digital machine nor easily understood from a reductionist perspective.

It is now estimated that there are 100 billion generally active neurons in the human brain; thousands of synapses per neuron; hundreds of active chemicals; and an infinite number of ways these elements can interact to produce specific behaviors.

Each brain cell (neuron) is connected to many others, and each is aware of what information is in these others. With Neural Network systems special microprocessors can have better access to memory by reading it as whole words, phrases, or graphic images, rather than unassociated bytes.

Being able to process information this way would increase their speed tremendously. How much faster do these neural network systems work? How advanced are they?

Mr. Sheldon Breiner of Syntelligence, Inc. is quoted as saying in 1987 "Maybe in 10 or 20 years there will be neuralnet computers doing fantastic things. But the technology is not nearly ready to commercialize."

Three years later, in 1990, Fujitsu Ltd announced a simulator with a capacity of 100,000 neurons.

Also in 1990, Hitachi announced a neural network computer capable of 2.3 billion operations per second. However, they do not define "operations".

While this technology is still new, and has a long way to go, it is the beginning of another revolution in the computer industry.

Humans being human, it will be used both to benefit mankind, and to find better ways to kill each other off in mass quantities, while keeping track of those that are still alive.

One such application for these systems is Optical Character Recognition. OCR is a method of scanning a page of type and converting it into a form that the computer can process. In other words, the computer can process the scanned text the same as if it were typed on the keyboard. Saves a great deal of time.

In 1991 NIST announced a new letter recognition program with 99 percent accuracy. One of the applications for this may be the consolidation of records.

All over the country, there are millions of pages of probate records and civil and criminal court files, old DMV records, birth and death records, and countless thousands of other documents stored in court house basements and warehouses.

Manually typing all these files into computer terminals is an impossible job; there isn't enough money in this poor economy to pay people to do it.

With this new OCR technology it may be possible to feed these yellowing documents into a high speed processor at hundreds of pages an hour. The new systems will read the information, classify, sort, cross reference, and file it away, to be made available to The Datanappers.

OCR, which presently works best with typewritten characters, is being developed to read hand printed letters and numbers. As this technology improves it will eventually be able to read handwriting. Read it and compare it with millions of samples stored in government computer systems. In California the signature on a drivers license has already been digitized, as has the photograph.

The Bell System is experimenting with neuralnet systems in the area of voice recognition, a technology that exists today, but it is far from perfect.

If neuralnet technology improves as some believe it will, computers will be able to identify a particular voice by comparing it with millions of samples stored in their memory. This can have some sinister applications. Any time you make a phone call, such a computer could recognize you and create a record of where you were when the call was made, along with all the other data that CAMA [12] stores. FBI agents could store voice samples of millions of Americans. [13] Then when "hippies and student radicals" demonstrate against the government, agents armed with tape recorders (instead of cameras) could infiltrate the crowds and make recordings. Later they could play the tapes into their massive super computers and a record would be made of who was there, which would be placed in their individual files.

Hoover would have loved it.

Neural Networking has other applications, some a little less insidious. Carnegie Mellon University is working on something called the Autonomous Land Vehicle In a Neural Network (ALVINN). The artificial intelligence capabilities of Neural Network computers are "taught" to recognize roads, trees, cars, etc. An ALVINN system using TV cameras for eyes may one day be able to drive the vehicle. Among other things, perhaps to deliver pizzas.

Lockheed has also been working on artificial intelligence programs to be used for driverless vehicles. They digitize thousands of photographs of things such as cars, and feed them into mainframe computers, to try to teach the computers how to recognize a real car from the live image from a TV camera. A fascinating new technology, but perhaps still a few years away. I recently spoke with Mr. Breiner, who is with a different company now. I asked if he still stands by the statement quoted earlier.

He does.

One day, computers will be able to identify a particular person's handwriting. Identify and also analyze.

While graphology is not an exact science, it can reveal a great deal about a persons character.

AND THEN ALONG CAME SEARS

Is nothing sacred?

Sears, so well known for decent prices and guarantees you can't find many other places, has been accused of selling a little snake oil of their own.

This is Prodigy, the database that anyone with a home computer can access for a small monthly fee. Prodigy was set up by the giant Sears empire in cahoots with IBM, and in the few years that it has been online, it has become one of the largest of these systems, with something like one and a half million users. When one subscribes to Prodigy, they are required to use the software they provide.

Well, not too long ago, according to some of the people who used Prodigy, something funny was going on. A file within the Prodigy software, called STAGE.DAT was allegedly found to contain names and addresses that were not supposed to be there.

Quoted from an article in Computerworld on 06 MAY 91: *"Users of the Prodigy videotext electronic bulletin board are finding text from personal documents in the STAGE.DAT file created on their hard disks by Prodigy upon installation."*

I talked to Mr. Bryan Ek at Prodigy, and he denied that they

intentionally uploaded information from their subscriber's private files. He did say that because of the way DOS is written that this could happen accidentally, but not because of the Prodigy Software. I decided to see for myself.

First I obtained a sealed copy of the Prodigy program disk from someone who had received it free with a new computer they bought. Some dummy names were made up and scattered throughout various files on the

hard disk drive, and then Prodigy was logged onto, running their program the B drive.

I watched the light on the hard drive to see if the software would access it. It did not.

The program was copied to drive E, old Prodigy logged onto again. Afterward I examined the STAGE.DAT and other Prodigy files with several programs. None of the made up names were found in any of the Prodigy files.

Maybe at one time Prodigy did take information from files that it was not supposed to be able to access. Maybe they did not. Based on my experiments, they don't now. I would not hesitate to use Prodigy if I were interested in it.

My point is that *any time you give any degree of control over, or access to your computer to anyone else, you have created some risk that this person might invade your Digital Privacy.*

A database that requires the subscriber to use supplied software could be set up by federal intelligence agencies. The software would be able to read everything on the hard disk drive, and could do a global text search for certain words or phrases. This system, however, might have an encryption algorithm built in, so the user wouldn't know what information was being uploaded by the database.

This is not, by any means, beyond the realm of possibility.

As far as other On-line Information Services, or *any* remote computer system that require you to use their software, consider a few things, if you will.

1. What do you really know about them?

2. Can you run their program from a floppy drive only, so that the software can not access your hard disk drive?

3. What do they have to offer that isn't available on another service that doesn't require you to use their software? Probably very little.

4. Is the source code available for examination?

I received a disk from such an online service, along with an offer of five free hours access time. Free, provided that I sign up with them...

I installed the program, and then examined the (many) files it created. In them was my entire autoexec.bat and config.sys files, which means that they apparently can examine them and see what programs I have a path to.

Knowing what programs I use, they can place my name on a mailing list to sell to whoever.

Not only that, but this program even copied information from the BIOS in my computer. Now what the hell do they need that for?

The Well and Compuserve don't need all this information about my personal computer. Why does this database?

I secure erased the files and threw the demo disk away.
Thanks, but no thanks.

Top: A single character as seen on the screen of a scope.

Bottom: The individual waveforms generated by each hey have slight differences. It should be possible to intercept the transient signal from a keyboard from a distance and extract the intelligence from it.

I would like to hear from anyone who has had experience with this technique, and any other area of transient interception.

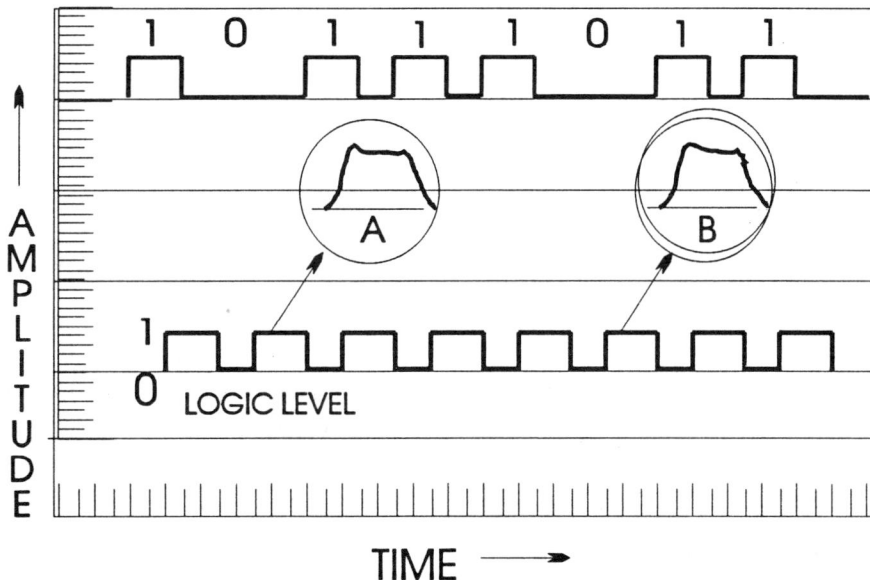

If what you have read so far isn't enough, there are even more ways The Datanappers can invade your Digital Privacy. The next section is about the van Eck method of intercepting information from your computer.

The van Eck Monitor Monitor

You're out partying with the guys, and find that you are a little short of cash when it comes time for you to buy the next round. Rather than having them razz you about it, you head for the nearest ATM to get a handful of twenties.

Job related stress has gotten to you, so you go see your Friendly Neighborhood Shrink (FNS) who prescribes "something to relax you."

A guy you know gives you a tip on a certain stock. "It's gonna go way up and you can get in on the ground floor and make a killing" he tells you. So you trot off to Schwab or Merrill Lynch and plunk down your life savings in the hope of making said killing.

Your wife has become distant and uncommunicative, but you are so busy with your job, drinking buddies, stockbroker, and shrink appointments, that you don't notice.

You also are not aware that she has hired a private detective to follow you around and see what information he can come up with.

Now this gumshoe is not the amateur variety that graduated from the Eastern Institute of Private Detectery located in a Post Office Box. He is a real pro, and among the electronic goodies that no real pro would be without is a professional van Eck computer monitor monitor.

And guess what your shrink, ATM, pharmacist, broker, and possibly your drinking bud-

dies all have in common? Right. Computers.

Said gumshoe is out there downloading all sorts of juicy tidbits about your personal life which he will put in a report that he sells to your dearly beloved. Your secret bank account balance, the name of the drug your shrink prescribed, and the secret love letters you are writing to your mistress on your home computer.

Whatever happened to fountain pens and perfumed stationery?

This information, coming from the computers the pharmacist and the bank and the others are using, is being broadcast to anyone who has the equipment to tune in on it.

Does this really work? Can people really do that?

You might recall what I said about laser listening devices in Don't Bug Me. Or to quote Leo Jones of Fargo Labs, "They work, but..."

Electronic equipment that can intercept signals from computers really does exist, and it really does work, but...
Read on.

How it works

The image on your monitor screen, the same as on a TV picture tube, is "painted" by an electron beam that sweeps back and forth across it and flashes off and on to cause various parts of the screen to either be lighted or dark. The screen is coated with *phosphors*, minerals that emit light when struck by these electrons. As this beam turns on and off, it generates an electromagnetic signal called a "transient" that radiates off into space just like the signal from a radio transmitter.

This transient radiation can be intercepted by special devices made for that purpose, which are sometimes called van Eck systems after Dr. Wim van Eck who demonstrated the technique in 1984. Using this system set up in a van parked outside a Post Office in Holland, he was able to intercept information from one of their computers. So the story goes.

TEMPEST

Intercepting transient signals from a computer isn't as easy as it once was. Some of the early home computers were made without considering the amount of radiation they produced. Or so it seems. These old systems flooded the whole house with the stuff, sometimes making a family meeting necessary to decide whether dad got to use the computer, or the family got to watch Gilligans Island.

The RF was so strong it could even interfere with the neighbors TV. At first everyone blamed in on "those damned ham operators" so it took a while for some people to make the connection. But when they could read on their TV screen the letter that a neighbor was writing on his new home system, they started to get the idea.

The actual distance at which a computer can be received by van Eck equipment is supposedly about one kilometer or less, but with more sophisticated receivers and directional antennas, this could be almost unlimited. The feds are rumored to have installed computer monitoring equipment in satellites that can receive these signals from individual computers on Earth. If they haven't already done this, it is a safe bet that they are working on it.

The extent of this radiation was a matter of concern not only to people who resented their neighbors spread sheet interfering with reruns of *I Love Lucy*, but also businesses

and especially the government, who naturally didn't want their data to be public. It just wouldn't do to have We The People knowing what the feds are up to.

It took some time, but finally the FCC started classifying computers into types, and limiting the amount of radiation they could produce. This reduced television interference (TVI) and the distance at which transient monitoring was still effective, but it did not eliminate it.

What does, to some extent, eliminate transient radiation are computers manufactured under a set of standards called TEMPEST, which stands for Transient Electromagnetic Pulse Emanation Standard.

TEMPEST "Certified" refers to a computer that meets the standards in "NACSIM 5100A". This is the NSA classified document that spells out the levels of transient radiation that can be emitted by a computer, and the things connected to a computer, and still be safe from van Eck monitoring.

While We The People can buy TEMPEST secure systems, we are not allowed to know exactly how they work.

There are several different levels of TEMPEST secure systems. According to what I was told, the lowest level, which provides a minimum of security against transient radiation, is D; A1 is the highest and most secure, and the C2 classification is medium security. The systems sold to the general public and businesses are allegedly this C2 classification, and the A1 systems are apparently available only to the government. The person I talked to at Wang Labs refused to tell me about this. Or much of anything, for that matter.

I wouldn't be surprised if the feds can still monitor the TEMPEST secure systems that We The People can buy, but as I do not have access to these NACSIM documents, I do not know.

It's not just the monitor

The van Eck technology is generally known for intercepting the transient radiation from a computers monitor, which is why I call it the monitor monitor. However, any part of a computer system can emanate radiation that can be intercepted.

Some of these signals can be reconstructed back into the original intelligence; a scope can see the differences in the "signatures" of the individual keys, so if the keyboard signals can be intercepted, they can be decoded. [14]

The drawing below shows what some of the signals inside a computer look like viewed on the screen of a scope. The little squares that rise from the baseline are binary ones, and the baseline is a binary zero.

There are something like 1700 different federal government agencies that keep files on citizens. Many of these records are available to you under the Privacy Act. The Federal Register (available at some public libraries) publishes the names of these agencies, and basic information on how to get copies of your records. An untitled book I am working on will have a great deal of such information, and the ACLU has a number of free or low cost publications on the Privacy Act.

Van Eck frequencies

What are the frequencies of this transient radiation? In a word, many. They're all over the spectrum.

Most of the signals are so weak that they won't go very far; many of them don't reach across the room where the computer resides. However, some of them do have enough range for van Eck receivers to pick them up. If you have a scanner available, you can experiment to see where you can pick up your own system. (You can also hear these signals on the low end of the commercial FM broadcast band.)

A good place to start is in the VHF TV channel 2,3, and 4 area, from 54 to 72 and 76 to 88 MHz where the commercial FM band begins.

The band from 72 to 76 MHz is allocated to the federal government for radio navigation and voice two way communications. Below channel 2, from 50 to 54 is the six meter amateur radio band. The area between channels 13 and 14; from 216 to 470 MHz is assigned to a variety of radio services. Transient signals can be heard in all of these areas as a strange mix of AM and FM but is received better as FM, so if you are using a receiver that has switchable modes, set it on narrow band FM.

If a particular TV channel is being used in your area, as you tune, or scan, across the 6 MHz wide section of the spectrum that it occupies, you will hear a lot of buzzing sounds (video and sync and color burst information) and the sound portion of the signal.

This powerful signal will probably wipe out the transient signal from a monitor. Search carefully around the center of the audio and video frequencies. They are listed in the table below.

CH	AUD	VID	RANGE	
2	59.75	55.25	54	60
3	65.75	61.25	60	66
4	71.75	67.25	66	72
5	81.75	77.25	76	82
6	87.75	83.25	82	88
7	179.75	175.25	174	180
8	185.75	181.25	180	186
9	191.75	187.25	186	192
10	197.75	193.25	192	198
11	203.75	199.25	198	204
12	209.75	205.25	204	210
13	215.75	211.25	210	216
14	475.75	471.25	470	476
15	481.75	477.25	476	482
16	487.75	483.25	482	488
17	493.75	489.25	488	494
18	499.75	495.25	494	500
19	505.75	501.25	500	506
20	511.75	507.25	506	512

The signal from your computer may be heard as a low pitched buzz, a quiet hissing sound, or a pulsing whine, which is the cursor blinking off and on.

As you are tuning, punch a few keys on the keyboard and listen for a clicking sound. When you hear it, you have found your computer.

Should you hear this while you are not pushing any keys, you may have picked up someone else's computer.

While visiting a friend who lives in Silicon Valley, I set up my PRO-2006 scanner with his outside antenna, and I could pick up dozens of data signals. A lot of people in that area aren't using TEMPEST systems.

Write down the frequencies and keep looking, until you find the strongest of the many signals you will hear. You can separate the strong from the weak by moving the receiver away from the computer, removing the an-tenna, or backing off the squelch to reduce the sensitivity. This record will be needed if you decide to build a van Eck jamming transmitter.

The strongest signal from this system (A 386 with SVGA monitor) is on 72.165 MHz, with others at about the same strength at 76 and 79 MHz.

Other components were received on various frequencies; printers in the VHF area from 30 to 40 and 140 to 200; and also UHF. The Laser Jet III comes in strong on 447.540; disk drives can be heard in the 72 MHz area and other places up to 200; and modems are all over the spectrum from the Citizens Band area at 27 MHz up to high VHF near 300 MHz.

Where to get monitor monitors

"OK", you say, "You got me interested. Where can I get one of these van Eck receivers"? Transient radiation monitors come in three flavors; government, commercial and home made.

Commercial systems

The professional models use a lab quality wide band communications receiver to pick up the signal. Such receivers have better selectivity and are much more sensitive that a TV set. The greater the sensitivity, the greater the distance from which it can intercept the signal.

Then this signal is processed through some sophisticated equipment which analyzes and converts it into a form that can feed into a computer. The captured image is viewed on the computer screen. Professional receivers for monitoring monitors are made by
Datasafe
33 King Street
Cheltenham, UK
Tel: 0242 573649.

Prices are from about 6500 to 12,500 British pounds, depending on the size of the screen.

I don't know if they restrict their sales. I have written to them twice and not received an answer. If you are interested, I know where there is a used commercial system for sale for about US $4000.

The other type of commercial system is a modified TV set, similar to what you can build. These are sometimes called SYN-REST systems, because they RESTore the missing SYNc signals. More on this.

Consumertronics Co. at 2011 Crescent Dr. PO Drawer 527, Alamogordo, NM 88310 sells such a van Eck system. It goes for about $1000.

Home made systems

If you have a black & white TV with a fine tuning control you might be able to see the transient signals generated by your computer.

Turn it on and load up some text on the screen. Now place the TV near the computer, and set it on whatever channel corresponds with the frequencies you have written down. Slowly, carefully adjust the fine tuning, and you may see the image from your computer screen on the TV. If you don't see it, work your way up through the higher VHF channels and then try UHF up to channel 20.

The image will probably be so distorted that you can barely tell what it is, but it might be readable. Depends on the type of monitor you have. You may also see fuzzy black bars floating up and down the screen.

The audio will probably come through much better, so if you punch a few keys you should be able to at least verify that it is your own computer you are receiving.

The reason the image is distorted is because of something called sync, or rather lack of

sync. Sync (synchronization) is the name given to the internal signals a TV set uses to stabilize the picture. There are two of these, vertical and horizontal. They correspond to the vertical and horizontal hold controls on a TV set. When you adjust them, you are actually adjusting these sync signals. Adjusting them might stabilize the image somewhat.

Now the monitor that you want to monitor also has sync signals, but as in a TV, they are at very low frequencies compared to the transient signals that contain the information on the monitor screen.

These low frequencies don't radiate very far, so the signal the van Eck device receives doesn't contain them. Also, they aren't at the same exact frequencies as the ones in a TV. This is why the image is likely to be unreadable, and why it is necessary to build a device to generate those missing signals; an external sync generator.

This generator does not have to be a very complicated device, essentially it is nothing more than two oscillator circuits that can be adjusted to different frequencies. The output of them is combined and injected into the TV set.

The circuits used in commercial systems are a little more elaborate. They may have rotary "thumbwheel" switches to set the frequency to where the operator wants it, and have a built in frequency counter.

Others are synthesized so the operator can set the frequency from a keyboard, the same as a programmable scanner. It is not necessary to be this elaborate, but the device will need to generate signals that can be varied in frequency. The frequency counter is a nice accessory, but it is not necessary to know what the actual frequency that stabilizes the image is; all that matters is that it works.

Generating SYNC signals

Consumertronics also sells a set of plans called "Beyond van Eck Phreaking". This booklet contains, among other things, a schematic diagram of a sync generator. It is not a project for beginners; some knowledge of digital electronics is required. The components include a dozen or so integrated circuits, seven crystals, switches, and various resistors and capacitors.

Also in the booklet are diagrams showing how and where to inject the signals from the generator into a TV set.

This booklet, 16 pages, seems a little overpriced at $29.95 but if the circuit works, it is a small price to pay. I have not yet built it.

Looking at the main diagram, it appears that the device will do what it is advertised to do, and the cost of the parts is modest; one could probably build it for about $50.

SPY Supply at 7 Colby Court, Suite 215. Bedford NH 03110 has a manual advertised in the latest issue of Full Disclosure which "Will show you how to EASILY build the [van Eck] device". The price is $79.95. I asked for a review copy, but they refused. I ask for details such as number of pages, types of plans or diagrams, but they refused this also. Considering the free advertising they could have had, I am skeptical. I'd like to hear from anyone who has purchased this book.

Some signal generators can produce the sync frequencies needed for van Eck monitoring. They are often available from surplus electronic companies. Check Nuts & Volts.

The cheapest way to make an oscillator circuit is by building it from a pair of 555 timers. This is a very basic system, all it does is generate two frequencies. It does not have switches to change them, which is why I suggested making a careful scanner search and noting the different frequencies found.

It also does not have a blanking oscillator or pulse shaper, and it lacks the stability of a crystal oscillator so the image may not be as clear as it would be using a more sophisticated generator.

Now the good part. This thing actually works, and if you dig around in electronic surplus stores for the parts, you will be able to build it for less than five bucks.

There are two ways to inject the signals into the TV. They can go into the antenna input or can be injected into the TV at the output of the video amplifier. Injecting the signal directly into the video section requires that you have, and be able to read, the schematic diagram of the TV you are using. If the TV you plan to use has no diagram (most don't) it may be in the Sams Photofact manuals available at most libraries. Write down all of the numbers you can find on the back of the set and take them with you. These numbers tend to be a bit cryptic, but the reference librarian can translate them for you.

However, if you don't know what you are doing, you can easily burn out something inside the TV as well as fry the 555 chips in the generator. If you do not have electronics experience, consider getting someone who does to help you.

Using the antenna input doesn't work as well, but is much simpler. The output from the two generators goes to the antenna input through a "splitter", the same device used to connect two TV's to one antenna. They are available at electronics stores for a few bucks.

It is easier to build the oscillators on a proto board, so you can quickly change the components without having to solder them. You might also use an RC substitution box, which has a number of different resistors and capacitors inside, and rotary switches to quickly change values.

How well do these things really work?

Above, I quoted Leo Jones: "...they work but..." Here is what that is all about.

The professional models work quite well, the sync restore types, not quite as well, and this 555 chip device is very iffy. If you decide to build this simple oscillator, understand that it is a crude system, so don't expect the same results that you would get from a $20,000.00 commercial unit. The TV's internal sync signals have not been disabled, and may interfere. Also, it requires some patience in trying many different component values for changing frequencies.

Don't expect to intercept someone's system from three miles away with such a home made system. Or one mile. Depending on conditions, maybe a block or two. Maybe. Using a directional antenna will increase the range, if it is pointed directly at the target.

Then even if you can receive the signal, can you reconstruct it?

If you intercept an old system that uses a TV set as a monitor, you probably will be able to read it, but a television set isn't capable of the fine resolution that some monitors are. With a TV you get 525 lines scanning across the screen, but some monitors have more than that. SVGA monitors have 1024 lines. The TV just isn't going to reproduce such a signal very well.

Now the commercial systems are different. One in particular that I was told about was used to for experiments conducted at an Ivy League University.

The range, I was told, was "miles", using a "spiral log conical" antenna. They were also able to single out a particular monitor among a number of others in the same lab.

"We even worked out that it should be possible for a satellite to tune in on a computer in an isolated area like the middle of the Kalahari Desert"

Someone at a company that makes hard disk drives was telling me about one of their customers; the government of a mid eastern country. "They buy our drives because they are shielded so well", he said, and went on to explain that with the equipment the government uses, it is actually possible to pick up the RF signals of an unshielded drive from an passing aircraft.

While a SYNREST system that can be made for a few bucks will work on some types of monitors and at fairly close range, you have to spend some money for a system that will intercept a SVGA monitor from a distance of several miles. Commercial interception systems can cost tens of thousands of dollars.

If you read *Wireless Microphones & Surveillance Transmitters* "The Bug Book" you will recall that the range of a surveillance transmitter depends on the amount of power it has, the frequency used, the receiver, the receiving and transmitting antennas, and what, if anything, is in the signal path that could block transmission. The same principles apply here.

Also important is the skill of the operator. Knowing the equipment, using the right antenna, and patience, can make the difference between success and failure.

As far as the systems the government uses, who knows? They aren't telling...

More Trickery

Here are a few tricks a spy might use to improve on van Eck monitoring of your computer. If the spy can get access to the computer, he can install an RF transmitter, (and also a microphone) somewhere on or inside the system.

...We even worked out that a satellite 22 thousand miles up should be able to intercept transient signals from an isolated PC in the Kalhari Desert.

An Ivy League university professon as quoted on the Internet.

The basic sync-restore van Eck system consists of only the sync generator, a TV set, and an antenna. The VCR is useful for recording the intercepted information.

Much patience is required using this kind of system, in trying different frequencies and aiming the antenna,

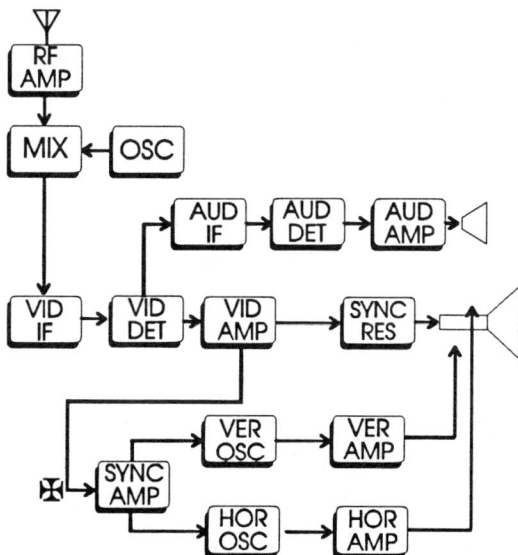

A simplified block diagram of a B&W TV set, showing the insertion point for the generated sync signals. They are combined through a "splitter" and injected into the sync amplifier stage.

The existing sync signals in the TV should be disabled. This requires some knowledge of electronic circuit tracing.

A microphone can be installed inside an external modem. While this isn't technically difficult, it takes time to pull it apart and do the wiring. How well it will work (or if it will work at all) depends. Some modems are connected to the phone line with four conductor cable. Only two of them are used. The other two can be used for the microphone, and can be tapped into anywhere along the phone line. This won't get information directly from the computer, but sometimes what the person operating it has to say will be useful.

An RF transmitter may broadcast signals from a computer with more power than the monitor. Meaning that they can be intercepted from a greater distance. The logical place for such a transmitter is inside the monitor, but installing it isn't the easiest job there is. If you have ever taken one of the damn things apart, you know what I mean. It takes time. Which a spy might not have.

> *In **The Bug Book**, I suggested that a spy might not have enough time to install a transmitter where it would have a constant source of power. So an alternative would be to damage something in the target area (a typewriter or a computer) so that it would have to be sent out to be repaired. If the spy can find out where it is being sent, he might be able to get into the repair facility and install the device.*

A transmitter inside the computer case is less likely to be effective; there are umpteen RF signals floating around there. Some will interfere with others, and the signal may be impossible to reconstruct even if it can be intercepted. The case will usually be made of metal, which will block the signal and reduce the range.

The keyboard is a better choice. There is constant power, it is away from the many RF signals inside the case, it is easier to get to, and there is plenty of space.

> *A very simple, and easy, way to prevent a spy from successfully installing and using a transmitter inside your computer is to paint over the screws that hold it together, with "invisible" solutions that glow under ultraviolet light. Use a battery powered UV light to check, you will see if someone has been tampering with your system. It only takes a few seconds.*

While a van Eck monitoring system has no control over what is being displayed on the target screen, a clever spy might be able to get the person who is using the computer to help them out.

A person working in the office of Wexlers Widget Works gets a call from someone who says they are the secretary of the accountant who keeps old man Wexlers books. There is a problem with the last quarterly sales report that was FAXed; it came out unreadable. They want another one. So the person calls the information up on the screen to print it, and the spy captures it on his VCR.

A spy might be in a situation where he can't get close enough to use his van Eck equipment. A van parked near the target area might be noticed, and someone might come around to investigate.

If he can get inside the room where the computer is located, there are things he can do to cause the target system to transmit a little farther. Or maybe a lot farther.

One day a clown (the real kind that wear a costume and hang around a circus) bounces into your office carrying a stack of coins in one hand and some leaflets in the other.

Before you get a chance to tell him that he isn't allowed in the office, he starts prancing around the room, acting like ,well, a clown, and then draws your attention to the coins, as if he were about to perform a magic trick.

Then he accidentally drops the coins on the floor. Some of them roll over to where some of the other employees are standing. The normal human reaction is to help him pick them up. Diversion.

Some of them roll under the desk. Where the computer is.

He gives you a coy clown grin, and crawls under the desk to get his coins, dropping a few of the leaflets on the floor to further divert your attention.

After he has retrieved his coins, he picks up one of the leaflets, points at it, drops it on the desk, and exits with some lack of grace.

Elapsed time maybe fifteen seconds.

The leaflet tells about a new restaurant (that won't really be) opening soon. It might have said "I just installed an antenna on your monitor cable so I can intercept the transient signals from a greater distance. A few weeks or months later, you might wonder what ever happened to the new restaurant, but more likely you would have forgotten about it.

Ridiculous, you say. Nope. Something very similar to this has been done in real life. For the money that professional Datanappers are paid, they can be very creative. It is natural to see a clown as harmless. This is the image they try to project, and they do it well. Maybe in some offices he would have been thrown out. Maybe not. How would the people where you work react to such a thing?

Have you ever watched Mission Impossible? OK, its TV, but there some gutsy and creative things happening. Like in the real world of industrial espionage.

Now if this antenna wire could be concealed, such as under the edges of the carpeting, and lead to something metal, such as a filing cabinet that is near a window, this would be a better antenna. If there were an unused TV antenna on the roof and it were possible to connect our piece of wire to it, or the cable leading to it, this would make a dandy antenna. In almost any situation there will be *something* which can be improvised as an antenna.

Perhaps said spy can't get inside the area. A coil of wire placed on the outside of the building will pick up transient energy from the monitor, and could be connected to whatever is available as an outside antenna. Or improvised.

Watch out for people who offer to inspect your TV antenna for free, window washers, itinerant electricians... Spies do not always wear fedoras and trench coats.

If you want to protect yourself from electronic surveillance, learn to think like a spy. Not a TV spy; but someone who has real life experience and imagination and guts. Someone who says the hell with the rules and the hell with convention and the hell with how others do things. These are the people who make it to the top in The Biz. If you are in the position where you have valuable information in your possession, and someone else wants that information, these are the kind of people you may be up against. Suppose they decide to steal your secret files. What will you do?

Prevention

So what can you do to prevent computer eavesdropping?

First of all, you can shield your system. Starting with the monitor, you can surround it with something metal. A copper screen will work fine. You can also place it inside a metal box, but be sure it has a little space for ventilation and maybe place a small fan several feet away. If you set the fan too close, you will see why I suggested several feet.

Shield the cables and the circuit board inside the keyboard. Make sure that the shielding material is not touching the circuit boards, and then ground all of it. Have a maintenance person or electrician check to make sure that the neutral side of the power line, heating ducts, plumbing, aluminum siding, etc, are all solidly grounded. Filters that prevent radiation from getting into the power lines are available from electronics stores, and can be built from the information in *Sources*.

You can build a small transmitter operating on the same frequency as the strongest signal your monitor is generating. In The Bug Book I have featured one of the best variable frequency surveillance transmitters available. It covers 70 to 130 MHz and has a power output of up to 100 milliwatts. This can be a very effective jamming device.

If you have two computers in the same room, you might consider that they will interfere with the van Eck receiver; confusing it with two different signals on the same frequencies. Unfortunately, this isn't necessarily true. Each individual monitor has it's own

characteristics, even among the same models, because the values of the components inside it vary slightly in value. Capacitors and resistors, are generally allowed a tolerance of 10 to 20 percent, and this can be enough to shift the frequency of the transient radiation enough for a sophisticated van Eck system to differentiate one from the other.

There are two SVGA monitors in the computer room where I work, both of which are the same make and model. I measured the frequencies, and they are different.

A spark gap transmitter with the unoriginal name "Old Sparky" can be used for wide band jamming. Complete plans for building it are also in DBM. However, as you are not trying to jam high powered transmitters all over the neighborhood, a very small one will do.

Lastly, you can buy a TEMPEST secure system from Wang Labs or any of several other manufacturers. HOWEVER Since the technical specs on how much transient radiation can escape a TEMPEST secure system are still classified, I would do some experimenting with a good scanner or communications receiver. This is not intended as criticism toward Wang, or any other manufacturer. I think that it is probable that government spy agencies have commercial monitoring systems that are capable of intercepting signals from even these TEMPEST secure systems. The rascals!

VAN ECK MONITORING AND THE LAW

Since there were no computers when the Constitution and the Bill of Rights were written, they couldn't have been included in what We The People are supposed to be able to be secure in. Whether this includes information being radiated by a computer is, then, subject to interpretation.

The existing federal laws that apply to surveillance and interception of communications are the Communications Act of 1934; the Electronic Communications Privacy Act; and the Omnibus Crime Control and Safe Streets Act. As far as van Eck monitoring, it appears that none of these three laws restrict or prohibit it, so it apparently is not unlawful.

Omnibus says nothing about transient radiation. The ECPA concerns, among other things, cellular radio and cordless phones, but it says nothing about transient radiation, and The Communications Act of 1934 was written before personal computers existed.

There are two key words here; *communication*, and *radio*. In the chapter Electronic Mail & the Law, are several definitions (from the ECPA) of what can and can not be intercepted. One of them, "electronic communication" includes "data" and "intelligence of any nature" but only when they are transmitted by a wire or a radio.

A computer is not a radio, and the transient radiation they produce was never intended to communicate anything to anyone. So, from what I have been able to determine, there is no federal law that prohibits anyone from intercepting intelligence from transient radiation. [15]

It is interesting that, so far, no one has introduced legislation that would regulate van Eck monitoring. The reason may be that the government does not want such laws.

Consider that if laws were passed that made it unlawful for We The People to use van Eck monitoring equipment, these same laws might also apply to the government. They might be required to obtain a warrant before they monitored our monitors. This wouldn't stop them, but it would mean that the evidence they obtained would have been done so unlawfully, and so not be admissible in court.

I suspect that in major urban areas all across America, there are vans full of Datanappers and electronic equipment roaming around and reading the data on peoples monitor screens. They may be federal agents, private detectives, or just people who like to snoop and can afford the equipment.

Yours does not have to be one of them.

WIRETAPPING AND DATA

Computer data can be intercepted from a phone line the same as can voice communications. For data, including FAX, interception, a high quality recorder is needed (I have used a Marantz PMD-200 on my own line with good results) and a digital recorder is even better. Remember that your data can be intercepted any number of places along the phone line from your home or office to the telco switching office.

Any time you transmit confidential information to another system, you take the chance of being intercepted. This is especially true in large apartment and office buildings where access to the phone connection panel is not restricted and multi-line cables loop through the building.

Another reason to use encryption.

One way the 555 timer chips can be configured as oscillators. Values of the resistors and capacitors are determined from the docs that come with the chips or any text on timers and basic digital circuits.

An easier way is to use either of two shareware programs that do the calculations; ELECTRIC.EXE or 555.EXE. Both are available for $6.00 from Lysias Press. Price includes disk mailer & first class postage.

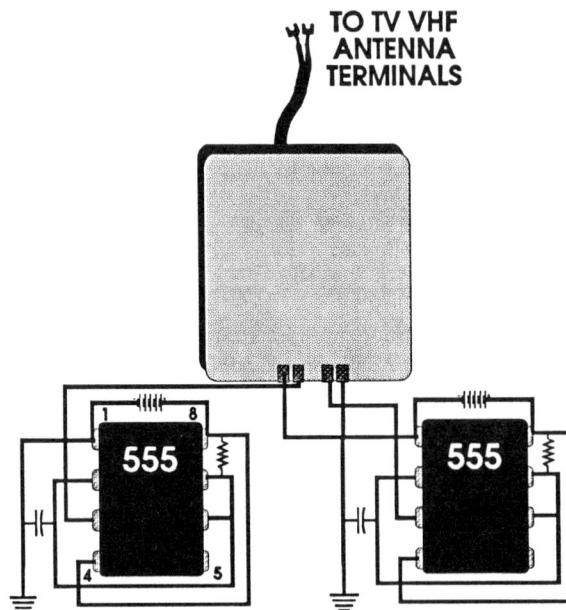

THE CELLULAR BROADCASTING CO.

One of the regulars on a BBS I used to log onto now and then, once posted a message telling about his experiments with using a portable computer to send and receive data through his cellular phone. Interesting.

Some other users on this system wanted to try to intercept it. So they took a scanner, frequency counter, and a digital tape recorder, and set out to give it a try.

They parked near his house and set the equipment up, then waited. (Some details are not included here)

Later that day, they "played" the data into a modem connected to one of their home computers. It came out almost perfect; there was a little garbage, but most of the text was recovered. While this method, using a scanner, works well, there is a better way. There are commercial cellular monitoring systems made for law enforcement agencies to use for court ordered surveillance.

These systems can be programmed with your cellular phone number, and whenever you use your phone, they automatically lock on and record whatever is being transmitted. Both sides of a voice transmission, or data from a computer.

If you use your cellular phone for transmitting data, you might consider encrypting it. Otherwise consider it intercepted and compromised.

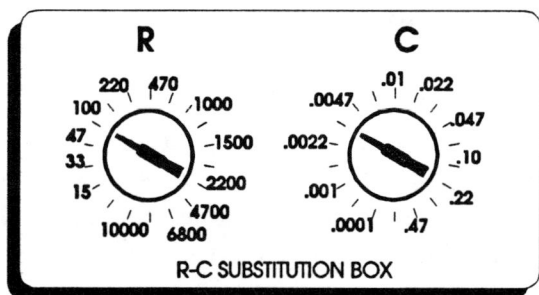

The R-C substitution box can be used to change values in the 555 timer. Most have a multiplier to increase the values by 10 and 100 times, and are available in most electronics stores.

NETWORKS & NOSES

Several years ago I wrote an unpublished article called "Networking and Noses" It was intended as a humorous look at the Internet; the difficulties new users have learning how to find their way around on it, and how the feds are said to intercept messages on it. The following is from that article.

Suppose you were to send an electronic mail message to a friend. In that message you make the following statement, "Well, this afternoon Deke and I finished painting his white house blue, so we went down to the capitol bar. I bought a shot of Old Redeye for Deacon and had a beer myself..."

Deacon was the Secret Service code name for a former president (Carter) and Redeye is a small hand fired infrared surface to air missile. The government's computer would zoom in on those two words, as well as *white house,* and within minutes the Secret Service would kick your door down and take you away, and no one would ever hear from you again.

OK, perhaps a slight exaggeration, but in reality, this isn't funny. The feds really do have programs they can use to search electronic mail for such incriminating phrases. Mr. Zimmermann mentioned this in his article.

If you use a modem to log onto computer BBS's, then you are probably have seen the warning usually posted about privacy of electronic mail. It says that private electronic mail isn't necessarily private. Unless you encrypt your computer messages, you can not be sure that no one else is reading them; you can be sure that someone else *is* reading them.

Back in 1984 (!) the FBI placed a series of ads in various newspapers and magazines.

These ads said things like "We're looking for computer literate persons to join the Bureau". According to Glen Roberts, the publisher of Full Disclosure, "They [the FBI] are desperately wary of the way information flows so freely in this medium." [16]

At the time, apparently the FBI wasn't too knowledgeable about computer data transmission, and they needed help infiltrating "this medium". The FBI is well known for their obsessive need to investigate anyone they consider "radicals or weirdos". (I have to admit that the FBI is right about one thing. There are some pretty weird and radical people in Cyberspace.)

In his article on government snake oil, Mr. Zimmermann predicted that one day electronic mail would begin replacing paper mail, and he was right. The use of electronic "E-Mail" is increasing at a fantastic rate. Between Prodigy, Compuserve, Netcom, The Well, and other fee based databases there are several million users who send and receive E-Mail. Many others use the Internet and UUCP nodes, which are usually free, and many more log onto "hobby" BBS's, nearly all of which have electronic mail message bases.

This presents some serious problems to government agents and other spies; it is now possible for people to send messages to each other without leaving a way to trace them.

Hoover must be rolling over in his grave.

E-MAIL & THE LAW

The Electronic Communications Privacy Act, section 2511 (2) (G) states: It shall not be unlawful under this chapter or chapter 121 of this title for any person--

(i) to intercept or access an electronic communication made through an electronic communication system that is configured so that such electronic communication is readily accessible to the general public.

As far as government agents logging onto a computer system that is open to the public, such as thousands of "hobby" BBS's are, it appears that they are free to do so even if they are looking for some illegal activities. They also can, apparently, use any information they find as evidence in court. However,

if such a BBS posts a conspicuous public message stating something like:

"This is not a public system. It is a private system. Only private citizens who are not involved in government or law enforcement activities are authorized to use it" then apparently it is not legal for them to do so under the ECPA. It is becoming more and more common to see this notice on BBS's.

HACKERS AND PASSWORDS

If your personal or small business computer is accessible by modem, there is the chance that someone might log onto it and download your files. It doesn't have to happen, though. This is very easy to prevent.

While much has been said about computer "hackers" [17] in magazines, newspapers, and TV news broadcasts, most instances of computer break-ins are never reported. There is more of this happening than most people realize.

In many instances, the hackers have some inside help. Not always, but often. It depends on the type of system and the security it has installed. If any. Some systems are fairly easy to get into, some nearly impossible.

One example was reported in Full Disclosure. Mr. Len Rose was convicted of "breaches of security" in computers that use AT&T's Unix operating system. [18] Many of the computers on the Internet are UNIX systems and breaking into them is not at all like other types.

UNIX is a much more complicated system than DOS and it takes some knowledge and experience to know how to use it, as well as knowing ones way around on the Internet. This too, is complicated. However, for someone who understands the Unix system and the Internet, it becomes much easier.

In such a system, the users passwords may be encrypted and stored in a file that is available to anyone who uses the system. At least as the Unix system is set up when it is sold to the end user, who has the option of changing this.

As many people still use passwords that are easy for them to remember, sometimes they can be unscrambled. Someone trying to do this has two things going for them: they are working with a very small amount of data (a

password may be as short as five characters) and some of them will inevitably be common words rather than randomly selected letters and numbers.

Using a spell checking program, Mr. Rose was allegedly able to enter various keys into a modified AT&T program called *Quest*, which is used to search the system for passwords that are too easy to break. He was able to obtain passwords that enabled him to access 18 different computer networks, including the NASA Ames Research Center in Sunnyvale, CA, the University of Maryland, and The DOD ARPANET. This is the Department of Defense Advanced Research Projects Network that shares classified research data among universities that are cleared for it, and contractors who are working on secret government projects.

Here is another example of cracking Unix systems.

In Amsterdam, Holland a small group of hackers got together to demonstrate their techniques, and the session was videotaped. This tape is for sale. The address where you can send for it is listed below.

First, they logged onto the Internet through a local phone number, and then used a system called Telnet with which they could connect to other systems on the network by typing in their electronic addresses.

Once logged on, they could access public file areas, open to anyone, such as the password file. Now in this case, rather than trying to break the code and obtain passwords, they make up one and insert it in the list. A few more tricks and it may be possible to replace the original list with the doctored list. The system will now recognize the new password.

Finally, they were able to access one of the many military systems in the US and obtain various files which included some documents dated 15 JAN 91, the last day for Iraqi forces to leave Kuwait. Sensitive stuff.

The last part of the tape shows how they then used the algorithm that encrypts Unix system passwords, and encrypted a list of common words and compared them with known, encrypted passwords, looking for matches. When they find one, they can use it to access whatever files the level of security the holder of that password permits.

These hackers did not damage the system, or destroy information. Nor did they disseminate classified information. They demonstrated how easy it was to log onto American military installations and access files. In Holland such non destructive acts are not criminalized; America is not that evolved. If the same hackers had tried that here, and been caught, they might have had their homes trashed and computers seized; been thrown in jail, and maybe fined enough money to keep them in poverty for the rest of their lives. Such is the awesome power of the federal government.

The Internet is such a huge system linking together thousands of computers of all shapes and sizes, that trying to maintain security is no easy task.

The Unix Tripwire

Many of these Internet nodes are Unix systems, as are many big business systems. As you have seen, they can be easy to get into. Something that may reduce unauthorized access to UNIX systems is a program called *Tripwire*, developed at Purdue University. It is described here from a message on the Internet:

Tripwire is an integrity-monitor for Unix systems. It uses several checksum/signature routines to detect changes to files, as well as monitoring selected items of system-maintained information. The system also monitors for changes in permissions, links, and sizes of files and directories. It can be made to detect additions or deletions of files from watched directories.

Tripwire, once installed on a clean system, can detect changes from intruder activity, and unauthorized modification of files.

Tripwire may be used without charge, but it may not be sold or modified for sale. Tripwire was written as a project under the auspices of the COAST Project at Purdue University. The primary author was Gene Kim, with the aid and under the direction of Gene Spafford (COAST director).

Copies of the Tripwire distribution may be ftp'd from ftp.cs.purdue.edu from the directory ub/spaf/COAST/Tripwire.

The distribution is available as a compressed tar file, and as uncompressed shar kits. The shar kit form of Tripwire version 1.0 will also be posted to comp.sources.Unix on the USENET. No mailserver access currently exists for distribution, although we expect some archive sites with such mechanisms will eventually provide access. Questions, comments, complaints, bugfixes, etc may be directed to: genek@mentor.cc.purdue.edu (Gene Kim) spaf@cs.purdue.edu (Gene Spafford) END

Other systems are not so easy to hack. Some are set up so that they require a series of access codes and passwords to even enter the system. If they are not entered correctly in the first three or so tries, the system will disconnect the caller. Once on these systems, you don't have access to a password file, and you can't use the tricks from the above examples.

Some computers used by the federal government are set up so that if repeated attempts are made to access them, things will happen.

They have ANI which means that the number of the line from which the call was made, and where it is located, are known to the system the instant the connection is made. Someone may go out to investigate.

There are very high security systems that require voice recognition by someone personally known to the caller as well as passwords. Still others require several passwords, one of which is changed every day, such as the COSMOS system used by Pacific Bell. [19]

The Private Hobby BBS

Now consider a typical "hobby" type BBS; a system set up usually by one person in their home for non commercial purposes.

When one logs on it usually asks for a user name, then a password, and sometimes the last four digits of their phone number.

Suppose I wanted to log onto one of these BBS's under another users ID. I already have their user name. Next I need their phone number, which may or may not be easy to get. If this is a system where people use their real names, and said person has a published number, then getting it is no problem.

If they have an unlisted number, and I don't know their real name, or their address, how am I going to get it? Without inside info, there is no way I can.

Now even if I get the phone number, there is still the password to crack. Some people use very long ones. An example of a long password once used by a friend of mine is "CamptownRacessingthissongDooDahDoo Dah". Actually, there are a different set of words to this song which were used in this case, but you get the idea.

Such a password is virtually impossible to crack. It has 37 letters, which could be arranged in millions of different combinations.

So, OK I log on using their name and the system asks for a password. I enter the first one I am going to try. Wrong, it says, try again. So I try again, and then a third time, but by now the system is tired of playing games, so it disconnects me.

All of the dozens (hundreds?) of BBS's that I have been on over the years work like this. There is just no way to log on as another user, other than getting lucky and hitting the right characters. That is always possible; that the passwords I try might belong to some other user, but if long passwords are required on this system, even that is unlikely. A five digit password using only letters has more than 10 million possible arrangements.

Most hobby BBS's have at most a few hundred users, but let's suppose a particular one had 1000. 10 million divided by 1000 is 10,000. So there should be one chance in 10,000 of hitting a valid password.

If it takes one minute to log on and get to the password prompt, 10,000 tries would require about a week, dialing continuously 24 hours a day.

This assumes that for a week, none of these 1000 other users are accessing the system, and the line is never busy. In reality, on some systems it can take hours of redialing to get through just one time.

Now even if I were to be able to find a valid password, it still might not work, because the real user of that password may well have used up his allowed time for that day, in which case I wouldn't get on at all. Chance I take...

Finally, If I were to do something I wasn't supposed to do, the system operator would probably notice it and cancel the password. The real user would have to get a new one, and I would be back at square one. Many, if not most, hobby BBS's are on a dedicated computer which sits right next to the sysops personal computer, and he can see what is going on whenever he is there, which for most of us is most of the time.

Of course the easy way to get on such systems is to simply log on as a new user, and ask for a password. Few of them bother to verify users phone numbers.

This will get you on, but it won't get you into restricted areas.

Business Systems

Another type of system is often very easy to get into. Big businesses who use "mini" computers; systems that are larger than personal computers, but smaller than mainframes, often are careless about security.

Many of these systems are accessible by modem so that branch offices, and employees who work at home, can log on to them.

I have seen electronic mail on a number of BBS's in which users relate their experiences accessing these systems. In one example, a number of people were using the electronic mailbox system of a large manufacturing company to send messages to each other. A very secure way to communicate. [20]

Many of these systems use the same logon procedure for everyone and some even the same password, giving a hacker instant access. Some areas, that contain sensitive data, are restricted by different access codes. These are, like the hobby BBS's, next to impossible to get into. Meanwhile most of the rest of what is in the system is very easy to get to.

An Unbreakable System

What does it take to make a computer 100% safe from The Datanappers? Here is a quote by Gene Spafford of Purdue University.

"The only system which is truly secure is one which is switched off and unplugged, locked in a titanium lined safe, buried in a concrete bunker, and is surrounded by nerve gas and very highly paid armed guards. Even then, I wouldn't stake my life on it."

A Breakable System

Now consider some comments from a person in the security consulting business, received by electronic mail. (Some of the text has been deleted)

Message #8963 - Phones (NN) (Received)

Date: 11-11-92 10:11
From: ********
To: *********
Subject: *****
Replies: #7462

Q1: Hobby BBS's that use passwords are all but impossible to break into without inside information, right?

A1: Depends. They get users *somehow*. It's possible to fake "credentials" and get on *any* system. Maybe not by using someone else's password, but by getting a new password yourself.

Getting access to a *sysop-level account* is all but impossible on most systems except the _____ of old,

(_____ is a local BBS that once used an early version of the WWIV operating system that was easy to hack.)

Q3: Is it true that UNIX systems are the easiest to get into (through the Internet e.g.) because there are so many of them, they are so big, and security is both lax and next to impossible on such large systems.

A3: Security is lax on many systems. On one system that I had legit access on they changed the new password feature to (1) require a password change at least once every three months, (2) all new passwords had to be at least 6 characters long and (3) all new passwords had to contain at least one character and at least one digit. This simple change eliminates the usefulness of just about any "password-hacking" type software and eliminates other methods of getting someone's password. *It's so simple I'm surprised most installations don't do this, but they don't.*

Q5: Large businesses using mini's are often easy to get into and there is a lot of this happening. Security is lax and they often don't change access codes. True?

A5: True. I often spot lax security measures concerning computer access with the companies I consult with. Sometimes they refuse to fix the problems even when I point them out, stating "that's not much of a risk."

One company put a modem on one of their computers on a Novell network along with _____(a software program). The ___ account was a supervisor-level account since the only people using it were me and their head of computer ops.

They didn't change the default password. Their LAN is on 24 hours a day and is tied in to their UNIX system, which, among other things, authorizes payroll and other direct payments by hooking up with their bank's computer.

When I pointed out that this was probably NOT a good idea I was told "we don't publish the telephone number that the modem is hooked to." As if THAT meant the thing was secure.

I changed the __ passwords to non-default passwords and made it only work in call-back-mode, then changed the __ account to a limited account that could only access __ and the login script, so anyone calling in will have to log-in before getting anywhere within the system. I told their computer ops guy what I had done and why and he still thinks that it was "secure enough before." The idiots.

In computer and news magazines, trade journals, newspapers, and on TV, you hear these big corporations crying about "teen-age hackers and college students" breaking into their systems. They complain about damage to, and theft of, files, loss of confidential information, and whatever else. "This is costing us millions", they say.

More often than not, it is their own fault for making it so easy, but naturally they want to blame someone else rather than admit it. As long as people are this careless, they can expect to have their systems invaded by The Datanappers.

HOW THE HACK DO I?

Suppose you want to try hacking. Just to see what it is like. Where do you start? First you need some phone numbers.

There are a few BBS's scattered across this country that have lists of modem numbers for businesses large and small, some "not so public" BBS's, and government agencies. Most of them are very old, and the numbers were changed long ago, but there are a few "live" ones. New lists are posted now and then.

However, this does not mean that you will be able to get to them. They may have such information hidden behind "doors" that the casual user will never see, or even know is there.

Perhaps after you have been on one of these systems for a while, others may begin to trust you, and some of these doors will be opened for you.

Much of the really good information is like the really good job openings. They rarely are advertised in newspapers, and are spread only by word of mouth. Get to know to users on the right BBS, and go to the meetings they have. These are usually at places that serve mediocre pizza. Attend and see what you can find out.

If and when you do get some numbers, you can try them and see what happens. Just keep in mind that there are laws that restrict what you can and can not do.

If you log onto a system and see a warning that it is not open to the public, that it is restricted to certain users, then you may be in violation of one law or another. If you want to avoid problems, log off without delay.

Several years ago I found a number on some BBS or other, and called to see what it was.

When it connected, there were some cryptic phrases and odd characters on the screen, along with the log on prompt. So I tried the usual stuff such as *guest*, *new*, *new user*, *help*, and like that (which didn't work) and then I happened to notice the letters BATF in the lower right corner of the screen. Bureau of Alcohol, Tobacco & Firearms. Treasury Department. Feds. I did a drop carrier real quick and didn't call back.

If you do not have a way of getting hackable numbers, you can use a "War Games" dialer.

War Games Dialers

As in the movie, a "War Games" dialer, sometimes called a *Demon Dialer* is a program that can be set up to automatically dial phone numbers, looking for other computers to communicate with. Or maybe break into. [21]

Not so many years these dialers were hardware devices that sold for several hundred dollars, and would dial sequential numbers only. Today they are software programs, and can be downloaded free from hundreds of BBS's. The better ones are non sequential.

A few of them that are available for free download on some BBS's are A-Dial, F-Hack, Aspen, Ultra-Dial, and others.

If you use one of these dialers, here are some things that you will be up against.

Overlord

One is a system called Overlord. Phone companies have regulations against using sequential dialers, but they aren't usually enforced. If they were, we would get fewer calls from Telemarketing companies trying to sell us things we would already have if we really wanted them.

Overlord is triggered when more than a certain number of sequential phone numbers are called from one line, and a printer prints out a record of it.

So if you use a sequential dialer, the telco will have a record of the calls you made.

CAMA

Hackers can avoid being flagged by Overlord by using a non sequential dialer. This kind of dialer is first programmed with a prefix, and then it will randomly select the last four digits to be dialed.

This may defeat Overlord, but there is still CAMA.

CAMA is an acronym for Centralized Automated Message Accounting, a system that keeps a computer tape record of every call made from every phone in the system.

These records can be accessed by telco security and law enforcement, and in the event of some major system break-in they will show where the calls originated. If there is a breach of security in your business system, you may have your attorneys look into obtaining CAMA records.

I have heard that telco keeps these tapes for six months, but don't know for sure. They won't tell me.

Traps & Pen Registers

Another security measure people can take is to have telco security install a *trap* on their line.

This trap, once called a "Pen Register" will keep a record of every call that comes in to their number, the number that made the call, and the time of the call.

If someone is making repeated attempts to access your system, you can arrange for the telco to set it up.

If you call the telco and ask them about CAMA, they will probably tell you they never heard of it. I tried this myself, and could not find anyone in administration or security that would admit that there is such a thing. There is.

What's a Hacker To Do?

There are many different ways to catch a hacker, but there are also ways to get around them.

One was demonstrated on Sixty Minutes a few weeks ago, in the story of organized betting on sporting events. If you have the funds, and know how to trace phone wires, then you can rent an apartment somewhere and have phone service installed. Then you tap the incoming line, at a remote location (called an *appearance)* and lead it to where you set up the hacking operation. [22] If the activities are discovered through CAMA or OVERLORD and someone comes out to investigate, all they find is an empty apartment. It won't take the telco very long to trace the line to where it is tapped, but there are alarm systems that can be used to warn the hackers that this is happening. See *Sources.*

The same system can be used if someone were to arrange to have a phone line installed in a vacant apartment in the building they live in, and then tap into it. As a security measure, they can rig the tap wires so that they pull loose if the cover to the connection panel is opened.

Using a cellular phone, while very expensive, is another way to avoid getting caught, *if it is done right.* [23]

On The Other End

So, as you can see, there are ways to catch people who try to access systems they are not supposed to access, and there are ways around these ways.

Either way, whether they get caught or not, if they get to your files then the information is compromised. What you need is something on your end to keep anyone from being able to get to your files.

Obviously, the safest thing you can do is turn off your computer, or at least the modem, before you leave your home or office. Supposing, however, you need to leave it on all the time. You might be a reporter who spends a lot of time in the field, and now and then you need to use a portable computer to log on to your home system to get information.

There is a very good program called Commute, from Central Point Software, that may be the answer.

First of all, you can set it up so that only selected callers can access the system. If the caller name does not match one of the ones in the file, they can't get access.

Next, you can set up a password access. No PW no access.

Finally, you can set it up so it will call back to make sure the caller is at the number that they are supposed to be at. If not, no access.

This way, even if someone knew that Joe Kalinski had access to your system, he would have to be calling from Mr. Kalinski's home number and have the password, or Commute wouldn't let him in.

Remember that with Commute, whoever gets access to your system has complete freedom to do anything on the system that they could do if they were at the keyboard. Such as deleting all your files, uploading a virus, and etc. So be careful who you let use it.

The "Auditor" from Millidyne, Inc. is a hardware device that plugs in between a modem and the phone line. It will prevent a hacking computer from hearing your modems identifying tone unless an access code is first entered. Auditor has the callback feature, and when the return call has been made, a second password is required from the other end. Very nice.

SICK SYSTEMS

If The Datanappers finally give up on trying to get to your data, there is still one thing they can do.

Suppose you were the inventor in the previous section, the one that is perfecting the radical new widget design. It is almost ready to patent and the competition is two weeks behind you. Possibly because most of his employees got tired of not getting paid, and quit.

At this point, old man Wexler will do anything to get ahead of you. So he arranges to get a virus into your system by sending you an infected copy of McGillicuddies newest version of Radical Widget Design software (RWDS).

Unsuspecting, you don't check it before you install it on your hard disk drive, and the next day all your research files are lost. The last time you made backups was three weeks ago. Wexler gets their widget patented first, you lose everything, and die a penniless wino in a skid row hotel.

A virus is a program, or the modification of a program, that causes your computer to do things that you would just as soon it didn't do. Things such as crash the system, erase files, or even wipe out everything on the disk it has infected. Some such viruses add insult to injury by flashing some dumb message on the screen such as "Arf arf. Got ya" after most of your files are memories.

Like a biological virus, a computer virus can reproduce; it can make copies of itself which quickly spread across a hard disk drive and floppy disks that are used on an infected system.

There are dozens of these viruses making their way around, and can come from any source. A free program obtained from a BBS or a commercial program directly from the company that produces it could contain a virus.

Some of the more well known are Jerusalem, and Columbus Day, and there was infamous Internet "worm". Some of them are designed to lurk inside a computer and then come to life at some time in the future. When the computers clock reaches that date, it becomes active. One of the most famous was the Michelangelo which made the TV news for several straight days. While TV news tend to exaggerate things, these viruses can indeed erase everything on your hard disk drive, and hundreds of systems were infected by Michelangelo a few months ago.

Where do these damned things come from? Unhappy employees or ex employees of software companies, unfriendly foreign governments, college students, anarchists, ill tempered programmers, or all of the above. Anyone who can program can write a virus, and those who can't can use special "virus writing" programs. Some of them are menu driven, and a few of the viruses that can produce are VCS, VCL, MtE, PS-MPC, IVP, TPE, and Genvirus. They are circulating around on some BBS's.

More than one person suggested that the Michelangelo virus was written and distributed by one of the companies that (for a fee) check peoples computers to make sure they don't have one. Or fix them if they do. I don't know if there is any truth to this or not, but a lot of people made a lot of money from that particular virus.

People who suspected, or just feared, Michelangelo could have had a low cost, or even free, program that would have eliminated the problem. From Mc Afee. When the next "new" virus threat comes around, perhaps you will remember this.

So what can you do? Use anti-virus programs to check every disk that you get, no matter where it came from. *Including commercial software.*

Then make backup copies of everything you have *after* your system has been checked, and reformat any infected or even suspected disks. Keep these separate from other disks, in case you should ever become infected. Individuals who operate hobby BBS's sometimes have a separate computer where files uploaded by their users can be put in quarantine until they are checked out.

Mc Afee Associates are the industry experts, and can provide you with everything you need to know about computer viruses. The number of their free BBS is listed below. They are also accessible through Compuserve.

Any of the products and techniques in this book can help protect your computer and your data, if you use them.

But why bother, you say.

It could never happen to me...

PART IV: EVERYTHING ELSE

The last part of Digital Privacy has odds and ends of information that may be useful or interesting.

Do You Need Professional Help?

If you have reason to believe that someone is monitoring your monitor, or has installed a listening device in your home or office, I can suggest three experienced TSCM teams that can provide assistance.

Sherwood Communications Associates, Ltd. has been in "The Biz" for many years, have experienced technicians, and will go anywhere to do a "sweep". Sherwood is also one of the largest sellers of counter surveillance equipment.

Contact Mr. Mike Adler
Sherwood Communications Assoc.
PO Box 535A
Southampton, PA. 18966
215-357-9065

Murray Associates is another professional company that has the latest equipment available and has been doing sweeps for many years. Mr. Murray has an interest in van Eck transient monitoring, and has done some research on it.

Contact Mr. Kevin Murray
Murray Associates
PO Box 5004
Clinton, NJ. 08809
908-730-8733

If you call either of these companies, make the call from a pay phone selected at random. Don't use a phone that could be compromised.

The third company, located on the West coast, likes to keep a low profile, and does not want their name published.

The owners of this professional TSCM company are former (retired) government agents with many years of experience, and they do sweeps for high security federal agency facilities, as well as businesses and large corporations.

If time permits, write to me c/o Lysias Press, using a made up name (I don't need to know who you are) and include the number of a secure phone, such as the unlisted number of a trusted friend who you have given the name to. Explain the situation to the friend.

I will arrange for them to make contact.

THE INTERNET

The Internet has been mentioned so many times is this book that a little information about it is in order.

The Internet is an international data communications network that connects other networks together. Developed in the sixties by the Department of Defense, and financed by the National Science Foundation, it connects several hundred different nets and tens of thousands of computers (of every type) together, for the purpose of sharing information. This includes sending and receiving electronic mail and transferring files back and forth.

The sites, or computer systems on the Internet are called domains, which fall into various classifications such as *.edu* (educational institutions); *.mil* (military installations); *.gov* (government agencies) and *.com* (commercial; businesses and large corporations). Anyone who has Internet access can log onto the computers at some of these thousands of sites through *Telnet,* which provides an electronic gateway to them through their individual addresses. Some of these computers are open to anyone who wants to log on, and others are restricted.

Within the Internet is something called USENET, which consists of a number of Newsgroups. A newsgroup is an area intended for discussion and opinions, and sharing information on a particular topic. There are more than 3000 of these newsgroups, on every subject one can imagine. One of the newsgroups mentioned often in this book is sci.crypt; the science of cryptology.

It is not necessary to have direct access to send and receive mail on the Internet, or to be able to read the messages in these newsgroups. This can be done through a number of local private BBS systems, at very low cost, or free. These systems are called UUCP nodes, which access the Internet to process messages. There are also the big commercial systems such as The Well, Compuserve, etc. through which you can send and receive Internet mail.

Each person on the Internet has their own unique address, made up of their user name and organization. If the new payroll supervisor at Wexler's were named Carolyn Martin, her address would be something like cmartin@wexlers.com.

My address is sspy@west.darkside.com. *Sspy* is the name I use, and *west.darkside* is the name of the site or domain that I call to send and receive mail. This is a UUCP node called Dark Side of the Moon. The last part, *.com* designates it as commercial. If you subscribe to one of the above on-line commercial systems, you could send mail to me at that address.

Direct access to the Internet is available through a number of providers. A short list follows. The rates vary, and can be as high as $10 per hour, or with some providers, a monthly or yearly rate. The most affordable is Netcom. The monthly rate is, for individuals, $20 and there is a one time setup fee of $15. No special communications software is needed to use Netcom, Q-Modem or Pro-Comm and most others will work.

ALTERNET 800-488-6383

ANSNET 914-789-5300 & 313-663-2482

CONCERT Network 919-248-1999

JVNCnet 800-358-4437

MSEN 313-741-1120

NEARnet 617-873-8730

NETCOM 408-554-8649

OARnet 614-292-0700

PSINet 800-827-7482

How can I learn more about the Internet? These three publications will provide you with the information you need.

Kehoe, Brendan
Zen and the Art of the Internet: A Beginner's Guide, 2nd ed
Prentice Hall, NY , 112 pages, $22.00

Krol, Ed
The Whole Internet User's Guide & Catalog

LaQuey, Tracey
The Internet Companion: A Beginner's Guide To Global Networking, Addison-Wesley

THE HATFIELDS AND THE MCCOYS

In an above section I mentioned that PGP (and Iris) use an algorithm that is owned by RSA Data Security, Inc. Iris is produced in England, but PGP originated in the US, where it is subject to US patent law.

This program has become the subject of a great deal of controversy on the Internet. So much, in fact, that a newsgroup called alt.security.pgp was created to handle the message traffic. Among the topics are: Does PGP violate the RSADS patent; is a person who uses it guilty of patent infringement; is this a moral or legal issue; is it legal to export and/or import pgp, and whatever else people on the Internet can find to say on (or off) the subject of PGP.

Following are two statements; one from Philip Zimmermann and one from RSA Data Security, Inc. If you use, or are thinking of using, PGP, please read them.

Patent Rights on the Algorithms

When I first released PGP, I half-expected to encounter some form of legal harassment from the Government. Indeed, there has been legal harassment, but it hasn't come from the Government-- it has come from a private corporation.

The RSA public key cryptosystem was developed at MIT with Federal funding from grants from the National Science Foundation and the Navy. It is patented by MIT (U.S. patent #4,405,829, issued 20 SEP 1983). A company in California called Public Key Partners (PKP) holds the exclusive commercial license to sell and sub-license the RSA public key cryptosystem.

The author of this software implementation of the RSA algorithm is providing this implementation for educational use only. Licensing this algorithm from PKP is *the responsibility of you, the user,* not Philip Zimmermann, the author of this software implementation. The author assumes no liability for any patent infringement that may result from the unlicensed use by the user of the underlying RSA algorithm used in this software.

Foreign users should note that the RSA patent does not apply outside the US, and there is no RSA patent in any other country. Federal agencies may use it because the Government paid for the development of RSA. Unfortunately, PKP is not offering any licensing of their RSA patent to end users of PGP.

This essentially makes PGP contraband in the USA.

Jim Bidzos, president of PKP, threatened to take legal action against me unless I stop distributing PGP, until they can devise a licensing scheme for it. I agreed to this, since PGP is already in wide circulation and waiting a while for a licensing arrangement from PKP seemed reasonable.

Mr. Bidzos assured me (he even used the word "promise") several times since the initial 5 June 91 release of PGP that they were working on a licensing scheme for PGP.

Apparently, my release of PGP helped provide the impetus for them to offer some sort of a freeware-style license for non commercial use of the RSA algorithm.

However, in December 1991 Mr. Bidzos said he had no plans to ever license the RSA algorithm to PGP users, and denied ever implying that he would. Meanwhile, I have continued to refrain from distributing PGP, although I've recently updated the PGP User's Guide, and have provided the design guidance for these new revisions of PGP.

Ironically, all this legal controversy from PKP has imparted a forbidden flavor to PGP that has only served to amplify its universal popularity.

I wrote my PGP software from scratch, with my own implementation of the RSA algorithm. I didn't steal any software from PKP. Before publishing PGP, I got a formal written legal opinion from a patent attorney with extensive experience in software patents. I'm convinced that publishing PGP the way I did does not violate patent law.

However, it is a well known axiom in the US legal system that regardless of the law, he with the most money and lawyers prevails, if not by actually winning then by crushing the little guy with legal expenses.

Not only did PKP acquire the exclusive patent rights for the RSA cryptosystem, which was developed with your tax dollars, but they also somehow acquired the exclusive rights to three other patents covering rival public key schemes invented by others, also developed with your tax dollars. This essentially gives one company a legal lock in the USA on nearly all practical public key cryptosystems.

They even appear to be claiming patent rights on the very concept of public key cryptography, regardless of what clever new original algorithms are independently invented by others. And you thought patent law was designed to encourage innovation!

PKP does not actually develop any software-- they don't even have an engineering department-- they are essentially a litigation company. Public key cryptography is destined to become a crucial technology in the protection of our civil liberties and privacy in our increasingly connected society

Why should the Government try to limit access to this key technology, when a single monopoly can do it for them?

It appears certain that there will be future releases of PGP, regardless of the outcome of licensing problems with Public Key Partners. If PKP does not license PGP, then future releases of PGP might not come from me. There are countless fans of PGP outside the US, and many of them are software engineers who want to improve PGP and promote it, regardless of what I do.

The second release of PGP was a joint effort of an international team of software engineers, implementing enhancements to the original PGP with design guidance from me. It is being released by Peter Gutmann in New Zealand, out of reach of US patent law. It is being released only in Europe and New Zealand, but it may spontaneously spread to the USA without any help from me or the PGP development team.

The IDEA(tm) conventional block cipher used by PGP is covered by a patent in Europe, held by ETH and a Swiss company called Ascom-Tech AG. The patent number is PCT/CH91/00117. International patents are pending. IDEA(tm) is a trademark of Ascom-Tech AG. There is no license fee required for non commercial use of IDEA. Ascom Tech AG has granted permission for PGP to use the IDEA cipher, and places no restrictions on using PGP for any purpose, including commercial use.

Philip Zimmermann (Boulder Software Engineering) is a software engineer consultant with 18 years experience, specializing in embedded real-time systems, cryptography, authentication, and data communications.

Experience includes design and implementation of authentication systems for financial information networks, network data security, key management protocols, embedded real-time multitasking executives, operating systems, and local area networks.

Custom versions of cryptography and authentication products and public key implementations such as the NIST DSS are available from Zimmermann, as well as custom product development services.

And now a statement from Public Key Partners and RSA Data Security, Inc. It is reprinted with permission of Jim Bidzos, President of RSADS.

Risks of using pgp

One should be careful about assuming that the documentation in electronically distributed software is accurate, especially where law is concerned.

There is much that the documentation of pgp does not tell you about patent and export law that you should be aware of. Some of the statements and interpretations of patent and export law are simply false. This note will attempt to offer some clarification and accurate information.

pgp seems to be an attempt to mislead netters into joining an illegal activity that violates patent and export law, letting them believe that they run no serious risk in doing so.

PATENTS

Patent law prohibits anyone from making, using, or selling a device that practices methods described in a U.S. patent. pgp admits practicing methods described in U.S. patent #4,405,829, issued to the Massachusetts Institute of Technology, and licensed by Public Key Partners.

Those who send signed or encrypted messages, post the pgp program, or encourage others to do so are inducing infringement. Under patent law, there is no distinction between inducement to infringe and direct infringement. You are just as liable.

Being aware of the RSA patent makes infringement willful and deliberate. Under patent law, a patent holder is entitled to seek triple damages and legal fees from deliberate infringers. While the pgp documentation suggests that you probable won't get sued, it doesn't tell you what can happen when patent holders assert their rights against infringement.

Free and legal RSA software is available. RSA Data Security has released a program, including source code, called RSAREF. This program is available free to any U.S. person for non-commercial use. Applications may be built on RSAREF, and freely distributed, subject to export law. An application that provides Email privacy, based on RSAREF, which uses the RSA and DES algorithms, called RIPEM is an example. For information, send Email to rsaref-info@rsa.com or rsaref-users@rsa.com.

NOTE: The pgp documentation states that PKP acquired the patent rights to RSA "...which was developed with your tax dollars..."

This is very misleading. U.S. tax dollars only partially funded researchers at MIT who developed RSA. The U.S. government itself received royalty-free use in return. This is standard practice whenever the government provides financial assistance.

The patents on public-key are no different and were handled no differently than any others developed at universities with partial government funding. In fact, almost every patent granted to a major university includes government support, returns royalty-free rights to the government, and is then licensed commercially by the universities to private parties.

EXPORT LAW:

PGP leads users to believe that it has circumvented export controls when it says "...there are no import restrictions on bringing cryptographic technology into the USA." You are led to believe that since you didn't import it, it's legal for you to use it in the US. The "no import restrictions" claim has been made so many times, many people probably believe it.

One would be well advised not to accept this legal opinion. While stated as if it were a well-known fact, the claim that "there are no import restrictions" is simply false. Section 123.2 of the ITAR (International Traffic in Arms Regulations) reads:

"123.2 Imports. No defense article may be imported into the United States unless (a) it was previously exported temporarily under a license issued by the Office of Munitions Control; or (b) it constitutes a temporary import/intransit shipment licensed under Section 123.3; or (c) its import is authorized by the Department of the Treasury (see 27 CFR parts 47,178, and 179)."

Was pgp illegally exported? Was pgp illegally imported? Of course. It didn't export or import itself. pgp 1 was illegally exported from the U.S., and pgp 2, based on pgp 1, is illegally imported into the U.S. Is a license required? According to the ITAR, it is. ITAR Section 125.2, "Exports of unclassified data, "paragraph (c) reads:

"(c) Disclosures. Unless otherwise expressly exempted in this subchapter, a license is required for the oral, visual, or documentary disclosure of technical data... A license is required regardless of the manner in which the technical data is transmitted (e.g., in person, by telephone, correspondence, electronic means, telex, etc.)."

What is "export?" Section 120.10, "Export begins:

"'Export' means, for the purposes of this subchapter; ...(c) sending or taking technical data outside the United States in any manner except that by mere travel outside of the United States by a person whose technical knowledge includes technical data; or..."

Is pgp subject to ITAR? See part 121, the Munitions List, in particular Category XIII,

of which paragraph (b) reads, in part, "...privacy devices, cryptographic devices and software (encoding and decoding), and components specifically designed or modified therefore..."

A further definition in 121.8, paragraph (f) reads; "Software includes but is not limited to the system functional design, logic flow, algorithms, application programs..."

PGP encourages you to post it on bulletin boards. Anybody who considers following this advice is taking quite a risk. When you make a defense item available on a BBS, you have exported it.

PGP's obvious attempts to downplay any risk of violating export law won't help you a bit if you're ever charged under the ITAR.

Penalties under the ITARs are quite serious. The ITARs were clearly designed to put teeth into laws that make exporting munitions illegal. It's unfortunate that cryptography is on the munitions list. But it is. pgp is software tainted by serious ITAR violations.

These points on patent and export law are straightforward and can easily be confirmed with legal advice. However, there are other statements in the pgp documentation that should not go unchallenged.

In pgp 2.0, the author says, "I did not steal any software from PKP." (PKP is the patent holder for the RSA patent.) Of course not; PKP doesn't make any software. However, not mentioned is a software product by RSA Data Security called MailSafe.

This product was first shipped in July of 1986. Features such as digital signatures on the program itself for verification, internal self-check for virus detection, compression of plaintext and ASCII recoding of encrypted binary files, direct and extended trust of public keys through certification, including the publisher's public key in the distribution, display of a message digest, security and password advice, and many others are in MailSafe and are carefully documented in the user manual. The authors of pgp have had a copy of MailSafe and the user manual since 1987.

There may be nothing illegal about using ideas from another product, but there's something dishonest about misleading people into believing these ideas were your own in the interest of recruiting "fans".

PGP calls itself "public-key for the masses." Even this isn't original. The September 12, 1986 issue of the Christian Science Monitor contains a page one story on cryptography, and discusses MailSafe. In that story, an RSA spokesman is quoted as saying "Mail-Safe is public-key for the masses." Reprints of this story were widely circulated in RSA press kits, and received by the pgp authors in 1987.

The documentation to pgp would have readers believe that pgp was the result of a noble desire to save everyone from an evil government threatening to deny rights to privacy; that users and distributors of pgp have little or nothing to fear from the patent holders, who, it is implied, are probably dishonest anyway; and that one shouldn't be concerned about export controls because pgp beat the system for everyone by having been developed overseas and imported legally. The facts simply don't support these claims.

NOTES

[1] It is in no way my intention to do anything to help "criminals and drug dealers evade the law." I am well aware that some of the information in my books could be used by such people for that purpose, but this would be on a very small scale. The fact that some may abuse it is no reason to repeal the first amendment.

Big time drug dealers and organized crime can afford to hire experts to set up secure communications channels and record keeping methods. They may pick up a few tips from this book, but for the most part, they don't really need it.

Small time criminals, your friendly neighborhood bookies, muggers, and bank robbers, have little use for sophisticated data record keeping, and secure communications. They don't need it either.

Criminals and drug dealers? No, this book is for the general public. The average computer user. The small business person. It is for people who want secure communications and private data, as we are beginning the transition from paper to electronic mail.

[2] There have been many instances where federal agents have been caught spying on people without a court ordered warrant, which the law requires. This has not stopped them, and it never will.

[2.5] As you have read elsewhere in Digital Privacy, it is assumed the DES has been broken by the NSA, if not other government agencies. This may have been true for a number of years. No one (who knows) is telling, but when asked if they, the NSA, had the DES designed in such a way that they alone could break it, someone who is in a position to know did tell me that "they would not have done anything to thwart their own efforts". I think this is obvious.

The NSA tried to prevent the RSA public key system from being adopted as a national standard, as reported in the Wall Street Journal 09 JUL 90; NIST announced that they were coming out with a "public key encryption standard" which seems to have fizzled out; and they (NIST) also came out with a message authentication code, that was scrapped when scientists at Bell labs discovered a weakness in it. Certain prime numbers were found to be much easier to factor. Finally, there was the Biden DeConcini bill. Such things do little to give We The People reason to trust our government.

[3] There is a nifty little program called Crypto Quotes Puzzle Game which has a number of newspaper type cryptoquote puzzles. It places them on the screen in VGA, with the alphabet to the left from which the user can select the letters to substitute. It works with a mouse, and even has a "cheat" feature, so you can peek at the answer one letter at a time. (Of course *I* never use it, but *some* people might). Besides being fun to play with, it demonstrates some of the early letter substitution methods. The source is listed below.

[4] "The first ten years of public key cryptography" by Whitfield Diffie; Proceedings of the IEEE, vol. 76, number 5, May 1988.

[5] The reason why the names Alice and Bob are often used in publications about cryptography is because a famous crypto expert (I think it was Dr. Rivest) started using them to make it easier to understand the exercises in text books and papers. Before that the letters A and B were used (like in law school) which were too easily confused with the letters A and B as used in a math formula.

[6] The price of $185 is not for one program that works on all these applications. Each

application requires a different AccessData program, and each one sells for $185.

[7] Hellman & Diffie believed that the chips could be produced for $10 each, and that given the decreases in price and increases in performance, that in ten years, such a machine could be built for $200,000.00.

I talked to an engineer at VLSI, Inc. the company that makes the 007 and 009 DES chips. The 009 (which can process 100 megabits per second) sells for about $30, and the 007, (capable of 200 MB per second) sells for about $350.00.

While they are cheaper in large quantities, the least they could sell the 007 for would be *about* $100.

This would be *about* a hundred million for just the 007 chips. Now add the cost of the other components, building them into a room size machine, and an enormous power supply, and the cost is perhaps $200,000,000.

The 009 might be as low as $10 (probably closer to $20) in such quantities, which would be only 20 million, which would reduce the total cost to perhaps 120 million.

It is also possible that the government has their own chip manufacturing facility, probably located in Singapore or Taiwan, which would lower the cost very considerably.

To the cost of the hardware must be added the salaries of the technicians and engineers and programmers required to operate and maintain it, repairs, or the cost of obtaining the files that are to be encrypted.

There is also the cost of the electricity to power it. The spec sheets for the VM-009 show an average supply current of 250 milliamperes (one fourth of a watt) at 5 volts. A million chips would require 250,000 amps, which, at 5 volts, comes to 1.25 million watts. If the power supply that converts the input AC (probably 440 volts) is 80 % efficient, the amount of power required would be a little over 1.5 million watts.

At ten cents per kilowatt hour, that's something like a million dollars a year just to power the monster.

[8] Anyone who read that article, or this book, will know better than to encrypt any documents that they receive anonymously or under suspicious circumstances, or anything that may be released to the public at a later date, without first making *significant* changes in the text.

[9] Where MailSafe generates a different key for each message sent, in the Local Encryption it changes keys each time it is used. To change passwords, exit MailSafe and log on again. When you decrypt, MailSafe will automatically find and use the right key.

[10] In a forthcoming book with the temporary title *Sources* I will have a chapter on data encryption which may contain reviews on programs that were not received in time to include in Digital Privacy.

[11] Loompanics Unlimited and Paladin Press have a number of books on burglary, locksmithing and safes such as *Techniques of Safecracking* by Wayne B. Yeager.

[12] Whenever you lift your phone off the hook, a function of the telco ESS (Electronic Switching System) computer called Centralized Automated Message Accounting (CAMA) stores a record of this on computer tape. It makes no difference if you change your mind and not make a call, only dial part of the number, or get a busy signal or no answer; all of this information is stored. For "statistical purposes only" of course. However it is accessible by law enforcement agencies. See Don't Bug Me for one example.

[13] Federal agencies could set up phony telemarketing companies which would use

the automatic dialers described above. They could be programmed to call a series of numbers they believed were associated with wanted criminals or political activists. To keep track of them. These voice samples (called voiceprints) are as unique as fingerprints, and could then be digitized, classified, and stored just as fingerprints have already been.

[14] If you view the signal on a scope, you can see that the wave form generated by each key is slightly different than the other keys. It should be possible to reconstruct the text as it is typed, by recording and analyzing it. As one can use a communications receiver, rather than a sync restore van Eck system, the distance at which the signal can be received is much greater. I would like to hear from anyone who has had some experience with this technique.

[15] While federal laws apparently do not place any restrictions on van Eck monitoring, other, local laws may apply, such as invasion of privacy. Also, possession of certain information might be in violation of various laws. There is also the possibility of civil action if one were to get caught. If someone were downloading the transactions appearing on the screen of a bank computer, there is most likely *something* the bank can do about it. And if someone were eavesdropping on a federal intelligence agency computer and got caught, they would find said feds to be very unhappy.

[16] One example of this is their recent request for $26 million with which to modify telco switching systems. This would mean they could more easily install wiretaps on equipment that uses fiberoptic cables and digital transmissions. This cost would be paid by the subscribers in the form of a small increase in our monthly bills. In *The Bug Book* are statistics on the number of court ordered wiretaps for the last ten years. A look at these numbers implies that they don't (legally) tap enough phones to justify spending this money. These wiretap statistics have some sinister implications written between the lines.

[17] The definition of "hacker" depends on who you ask. Intense debates take place every now and then on local BBS's and the Internet, with messages ranging from polite suggestions to some heavy name calling, about what exactly a hacker is.

One definition is anyone who breaks into computer systems only to obtain information. Another is a person who crashes the system, or infects it with a virus or damages it in any way they can, and another is a person who is hardware and software literate, knows about the innards of computers and communications, but doesn't try to get into systems they are not supposed to get into.

[18] In a letter to Full Disclosure, published in issue #25, Mr. Rose states that he did not break into the computer systems mentioned in the Full Disclosure article, and that he was never even charged with "penetrating" them. He further states that he had legal access to them, and that the program he was reported by Full Disclosure as having used was not a modified version of the AT&T Quest program, it was something that he wrote himself. What he was *apparently* sent to prison for was possession of proprietary information. Meanwhile, Mr. Rose has been released, has paid his "debt to society", and has advertised in Full Disclosure that he is available as a Unix Systems consultant.

[19] COSMOS is the telco computer system that keeps records of subscribers phone number, long distance carrier, cable and pair numbers, and etc. As it contains this information for bank teller machine alarm lines, and those of government agencies, security is *very* high.

[20] I am working on a new book, as yet untitled, which will be on personal privacy, among other things. In it will be a detailed chapter on secure methods of communication.

[21] Not everyone who uses an automatic dialer is trying to find computer systems to unlawfully access, nor do they all intend to destroy data or crash systems. Most people will log off if they see that they are into a restricted system. If not because they respect that it is such a system, then because of the security functions inherent in some of them that could get them caught.

Some people who use these dialing programs are looking for public access systems open to anyone that wants to call. A number of businesses and government agencies have such systems, which are sometimes found only by using automatic dialers. Computer systems that can be accessed by modem, including hobby BBS's and business and government computers come and go. Old ones shut down and new ones go on-line so frequently that any list of them is obsolete before it is even published.

[22] An *appearance* is a place along the phone line, between the telco switch (Central Office) and where the phone is installed. This can be a B-Box (bridging box) on a street corner, a splicing boot on a telephone pole, or in an underground room called a *junction point*.

Tracing a particular line can be done several ways, one of which requires inside knowledge; the cable and pair number. All this will be detailed in *Wiretapping and Cellular Radio Monitoring* which will be out later this year.

[23] Whenever a cellular phone is turned on it is in constant communication with the cell site equipment. This transmission can be intercepted by a modified cellular phone, a system access monitor, and commercial monitoring equipment. It is possible to pinpoint the location of the phone, which can result in the hacker being caught. There is also the record of calls made, as in CAMA. Ways to defeat these traps will be in Wiretapping & Cellular Radio Monitoring.

CREDITS

Part of the information on the history of ciphers chapter comes from the excellent help file on the Iris program disk. Iris is produced in England, by Mr. Peter Moreton of Digital Crypto.

The story of Mr. Rose is from Full Disclosure issue #24. Full Disclosure is published by Glen Roberts. Subscriptions are $24 for 12 issues. Sample copy on request. Write Full Disclosure at PO Box 903, Libertyville, Ill 60048.

The story of the hackers in Holland; "The Hackers Video" was originally published in "2600" the Hackers Quarterly, vol. 8, #3, Autumn 1991. The videotape is available for $10 or three blank VHS 120 tapes.

Some details of the German Enigma machine are from the documentation of the shareware program 'Enigma' by J. E. Eller, 536 Caren Dr. Virginia Beach, VA 23452

Part of the information on Prodigy is from a letter to 2600 Magazine.

Some of the technical information on van Eck is from several unnamed people who sent me electronic mail on the Internet.

Some of the information about the FBI and BBS's is based on "The FBI and Your BBS" by Glen Roberts, of Full Disclosure.

Details and clarification of information I had on ciphers was provided by a number of individuals on the Internet.

SUGGESTED READING

Electronic magazines

Phrack is an electronic magazine published periodically and posted on various BBS's and the Internet. If you have net access, you can have it delivered to you by E-Mailing phrack@well.ca.sf.us.

Phrack is also available for download on many private BBS's, and other networks including Fido and Nirvana nets.

The *Computer Underground Digest* is also an electronic magazine available on various networks and private BBS's.

Both CUD and Phrack have articles on phone phreaking, computer hacking, people who have been raided by the feds and updates on the consequences, the trials, etc; interviews with and profiles of, famous or not so famous hackers, and the like.

Books, Computer Crime

Bequai, August.
Computer crime / August Bequai. Lexington, Mass.: Lexington Books, c1978.

BloomBecker, Jay.
Cracking down on computer crime : by J. J. Buck BloomBecker. IN: State legislatures. Vol. 14, no. 7 (Aug. 1988)

Cornwall, Hugo.
Datatheft : computer fraud, industrial espionage, and information crime / Hugo Cornwall. London : Heinemann, 1987.

Leibholz, Stephen W.
Users' guide to computer crime: its commis-sion, detection & prevention [by] Stephen W. Leibholz & Louis D. Wilson. [1st ed.]. Radnor, Pa., Chilton Book Co. [1974].

Parker, Donn B.
Fighting computer crime / Donn B. Parker. New York : Scribner, c1983.

Sieber, Ulrich, Dr.
The international handbook on computer crime: computer related economic crime and the infringements of privacy / Ulrich Sieber. Chichester [Sussex] ; New York : Wiley, c1986.

Van Duyn, J. A.

The human factor in computer crime / J. Van Duyn. Princeton, N.J. :Petrocelli Books, c1985.

Vance, Mary A.
Computer crime / Mary Vance. Rev. ed. of P 1255. Monticello, Ill., USA : Vance Bibliographies, [1988]. Series title: Public administration series bibliography P 2355.

Wold, Geoffrey H.
Computer crime : techniques, prevention / Geoffrey H. Wold and Robert F. Shriver. Rolling Meadows, Ill. : Bankers Pub. Co., c1989.

Books, Cryptography

Bosworth, Bruce.
Codes, ciphers, and computers : an introduction to information security [by] Bruce Bosworth. Rochelle Park, N.J.: Hayden Book Co., c1982.

Bowers, William Maxwell
Practical cryptanalysis. [Greenfield, Mass.] American Cryptogram Association [1960 1967].

Boyd, Waldo T
Cryptology : beyond decoder rings / Karl Andreassen. Englewood Cliffs, NJ : Prentice Hall, c1988.

Brandreth, Gyles Daubeney.
Writing secret codes and sending hidden messages / by Gyles Brandreth ; illustrated by Peter Stevenson. New York : Sterling Pub. Co., 1984, c1982.

Chor, Ben Zion.
Two issues in public key cryptography : RSA bit security and a new knapsack type system / Ben Zion Chor. Cambridge, Mass. : MIT Press, c1986. Series title: ACM distinguished dissertations.

Clark, Ronald William.
The man who broke Purple: the life of the world's greatest cryptologist, Colonel William F. Friedman / Ronald W. Clark. London : Weidenfeld & Nicolson, c1977.

Foster, Caxton C.
Cryptanalysis for microcomputers / Caxton C. Foster. Rochelle Park, N.J. : Hayden Book Co., c1982.

Franksen, Ole Immanuel.
Mr. Babbage's secret : the tale of a cypher and APL / Ole Immanuel Franksen ; foreword by H.H. Goldstine. Birkerod, Denmark : Strandberg, 1984.

Harris, Frances A.
Solving simple substitution ciphers, by Frances A. Harris; S. Tuck. [Rochester, N.Y.] American Cryptogram Association, 1959.

Jackson, Keith M.
Secure information transfer PC encryption : a practical guide / Keith M. Jackson. Boca Raton : CRC Press, c1990.

Kahn, David.
The codebreakers; the story of secret writing. New York, Macmillan [1967].

Kahn, David.
Kahn on codes : secrets of the new cryptology / by David Kahn. New York : Macmillan, c1983.

Meyer, Carl H.
Cryptography : a new dimension in computer data security : a guide for the design and implementation of secure systems /

Carl H. Meyer, Stephen M. Matyas. New York : Wiley, 1982.

Nanovic, John Leonard.
Secret writing; an introduction to cryptograms, ciphers and codes, by Henry Lysing [pseud.]. New York, D. Kemp & Co. [1936].

Pierce, Clayton C.
Secret and secure : privacy, cryptography, and secure communication / by Clayton C. Pierce. Ventura, CA : Pierce, c1977.

Rueppel, Rainer A.
Analysis and design of stream ciphers / Rainer A. Rueppel. Berlin ; New York : Springer Verlag, c1986. Series title: Communications and control engineering series.

Salomaa, Arto.
Public key cryptography / Arto Salomaa. Berlin ; New York : Springer Verlag, c1990. Series title: EATCS monographs on theoretical computer science ; v. 23.

Seberry, Jennifer.
Cryptography : an introduction to computer security / Jennifer Seberry, Josef Pieprzyk. New York : Prentice Hall, c1989.

Shulman, David.
A glossary of cryptography [New York, Crypto Press] c1961.

Wheeler, David.
Data encryption / by David Wheeler. Cam-

bridge [Cambridgeshire] : University of Cambridge, Computer Laboratory, 1987.

Wrixon, Fred B.
Codes, ciphers, and secret languages / Fred B. Wrixon. New York : Bonanza Books : Distributed by Crown publishers, 1989.

Articles, General

Personal and private: how much security is enough on a microcomputer? (include related article on the small data center. by Peter Stephenson v14 Byte June '89 p285(4)

Build more secure networks with data-encryption schemes. (DBMS Report)(data base management system) (Column) by Joe Celko v25 Systems Integration Feb '92 p25(1)

Pair claims to have cracked encryption scheme.(Data Encryption Standard) by Michael Alexander v25 Computerworld Nov 4 '91 p54(1)

This security system dares you to hack away.(Information Processing) by Paul M. Eng Business Week April 22 '91 p100A(1)

Encryption pact in works: six vendors to standardize on common scheme. (RSA Data Security Inc.'s public-key encryption system) by Michael Alexander v25 Computerworld April 15 '91 p1(2)

Digital security signed, sealed, delivered (proposal for a digital signature standard) by Ivars Peterson v140 Science News Sept 7 '91 p148(1)

Industry standard proposed by US. is severely criticized by team. (Bellcore Inc. scientists) by G. Pascal Zachary 13 col in. The Wall Street Journal Dec 6 '91 pB3C(W) pA9F(E) col 4

Cloak and data: using secret codes to secure your data from prying eyes. (tutorial) by Rick Grehan v15 BYTE June '90 p311 (8)

FastLock keeps sensitive data away from prying eyes. (Software Review) (evaluation)

by Rock Miller il v8 PC Magazine Sept 26 '89 p51(1) Byte June '90 p311(8)

A new light on codes. (undetected light beams in cryptography) (column) by Pallab Ghosh il Management Today Dec '89 p120(1)

Scientists devise math tool to break a protective code. (Data Encryption Standard used by many businesses) (National Pages) by John Markoff il 15 col in. v141 The New York Times Oct 3 '91 pA12(N) pA18(L) col 1

Analysis of the Encryption Algorithm used in the Word Perfect Word Processing Program, Bennet,J. 1987, "Cryptologia" Vol XI, No. 4. pp 206-210

Data encryption protects data at PC level.(microcomputers) by Amy Bermar il v6 PC Week June 26 '89 p108(1)

Experimenting with an unbreachable electronic cipher. (cryptography and data communications) (Technology) by John Markoff il 36 col in. v141 The New York Times Jan 12 '92 sec 3 pF9(N) pF9(L) col 1

A cure for the common code: computer cryptography.v320 The Economist Sept 21 '91 p104(2)

Secret codes: any good data security system must rely on encryption. (technical) by Asael Dror il v14 Byte June '89 p267(4)

The conflict surrounding the data encryption standard. by Lawrence J. Aragon v21 Defense Electronics March '89 p108(1)

There's still plenty of life in that old spy stuff. (sales of encryption devices should increase from $3.3 billion in 1992 to $4.8 billion in 1996) (Information Processing) (Industrial Edition) (Brief Article) by Paul M. Eng Business Week Jan 20 '92 p86D(1)

Super computers

CPU firms seek wider market. (Intel unit offers high-end model) (Intel Corp., supercomputer) by Craig Stedman il v37 Electronic News Nov 25 '91 p11(2)

Cray will offer new computer at $30.5 million.(Cray Research Inc.'s Cray Y-MP C-90) (Product Announcement) by Hal Lancaster 9 col in. The Wall Street Journal Nov 19 '91 pB5(W) pA8(E) col 1

The NIST DSS:

Digital security signed, sealed, delivered.(proposal for a digital signature standard) by Ivars Peterson v140 Science News Sept 7 '91 p148(1)

Big Brother

Uncle Sam's secret decoder ring. (encryption, method of computer security, is strictly regulated by US. government) (Column) by Eric Hirschhorn and David Peyton il 19 col in. v115 The Washington Post June 25 '92 pA23 col 3

U.S.warns on advances in encoding, (defenses against wiretapping outpace Government's ability to monitor telephone communications) by Keith Bradsher 18 col in. v141 The New York Times April 30 '92 pC1(N) pD1(L) col 6

Biden bill raises fears for safety of coded data.(Joseph R. Biden)(Technology/Operations News) by Jeanne Iida v156 American Banker May 1 '91 p3(1)

U.S. Plan to restrict encryption software exports draws protests, by Evelyn Richards 10 col in. v114 The Washington Post Nov 14 '91 pB11 col 2

Paper on codes distributed over objections.(secrecy is pitted against academic freedom) (National Pages) by John Markoff 19 col in. v138 The New York Times August 9 '89 pA11(N) pA16(L) col 2

Agency dealt blow on rules for messaging. (US Computer System Security and Privacy Advisory Board recommends that US Department of Commerce delay adopting security standard) (Technology) by G. Pascal Zachary 10 col in. The Wall Street Journal April 6 '92 pB6(W) pB8(E) col 4

Data security plan bashed: federal panel foregoes popular RSA scheme. (RSA Data Security Inc.) by Michael Alexander v25 Computerworld July 1 '91 p1(2)

U.S. cryptography policy stunts client/server sales. (National Security Agency's regulation of cryptography technology required to make client/server applications secure) (Net Value) (Column) by Jamie Lewis v9 PC Week April 27 '92 p81(1)

PLACES TO GET THINGS

BCC
is at 1610 Crane Court
San Jose, CA. 95112
408-944-9000

BOULDER SOFTWARE ENGINEER-ING
is at 3021 Eleventh Street Boulder, Colorado 80304 Phone 303-541-0140 voice & FAX. (10:00am 7:00pm Mountain Time) Email: prz@sage.cgd.ucar.edu

COMPUTER VIRUS INFORMATION
Mc Afee Associates is at 3350 Scott Blvd. Building 14, Santa Clara, CA 95054 408-988-3832. Their free BBS number is 408-988-4004.

COMPUTER SECURITY JOURNAL
is published by Computer Security, Inc. 360 Church Street Northborough, MA. 01523 508-393-2600

CRAY COMPUTER CORPORATION
If you happen to have a few million that you don't know what to do with, you can buy a Cray. Cray Computer Corporation is at 1110 Bayfield Dr. Colorado Springs, CO. 80906

CRYPTOQUOTE PUZZLE
The cryptoquote puzzle game was written by Nels Anderson at 92 Bishop Drive, Framingham MA. 01701. A shareware program, registration is only $10.00 for which you get some additional puzzles, or for $20.00 you get the deluxe version with a manual and all of the puzzles.

DECO INDUSTRIES
makes the VT-75 transmitter that can be used for jamming van Eck equipment. They are at PO Box 607, Bedford Hills, NY 10507. Contact Peter.

DOLPHIN ENCRYPT
is at 4815 W. Braker Lane, #502 Austin, Texas 78759. 512-479-9208. Contact Mr. Peter Meyer

DOSS INDUSTRIES
is at 1224 Mariposa, San Francisco 94107. 415-347-2301

ENIGMA PROGRAM
The author of the Enigma machine computer simulation is J. E. Eller at 536 Caren Dr, Virginia Beach, Va, 23452

EXECUTIVE PROTECTION PROD-UCTS, INC.
is in the wine country, at 1325 Imola Ave. Napa, California 94559. Phone is 707-253-7142. The owner is Gene Kelly.

FULL DISCLOSURE
is at PO Box 903, Libertyville, IL. 60048. Contact Glen Roberts.

GLOBAL COMPUTER SUPPLIES, INC.
Global has four locations:

11 Harbor Park Dr, Port Washington, NY 10050
1050 Northbrook Parkway, Suwanee, GA 30174
2318 Del Amo Blvd, Compton CA 90220
2249 Windsor Court Addison, IL 60101.

LIBERTY SYSTEMS
is at 160 Saratoga Ave, Ste. 38, Santa Clara, CA. 95051 408-983-1127

ENCRYPT-IT
is available from MaeDae Enterprises is at 5430 Murr Rd. Peyton CO. 80831

NUTS & VOLTS MAGAZINE
Self described as "A National Publication For The Buying And Selling Of Electronic Equipment", Nuts & Volts is just that. An excellent source of new and used computers

and electronic gear, and a lot more. Write to 430 Princeland Ct. Corona, Ca. 91719. 714-371-8497. Subscription order only line is 800-783-4624.

PALADIN PRESS
You can write to Paladin Press at PO Box 1307 Boulder, CO 80306 or call them at 303-443-7250. Their 50 page catalogue lists hundreds of books.

PC GUARDIAN SECURITY PRODUCTS
1133 E. Francisco Blvd.
San Rafael, CA. 94901
415-459-0190

PRINTER WORKS
3481 Arden Road
Hayward, CA. 94545
800-225-6116

SECURE-IT
is at 18 Maple St. Longmeadow, MA. 01028

THE PRIVATE LINE
The Private Line DES program, is available from Everett Enterprises 7855 Wintercress Dr, Springfield, VA 22152 703-866-3914. This is a shareware program. Registration is $30.

RSA DATA SECURITY, INC.
RSA is at 10 Twin Dolphin Dr. Redwood City, Ca. 94065, 415-595-8782.

SHAREWARE
One of the largest sellers of shareware programs is PC SIG at 1030D East Duane Ave. Sunnyvale, Ca. 94086. 408-730-9291. Their catalogue, which costs $19.95, is on ten floppy disks and lists thousands of programs.

SUPER COMPUTERS.

Here is some information on super computers that you might find interesting.

The price of some Cray models:
The Y-MP8-128:$23.7 million
The Y-MP2-116:$5 million
The Y-MP8-432:$13.45 million
The Y-MP8-4128:$18.7 million
The Y-MP8-8:$18.45 million
The Y-MP8-64:$19.95 million

The very latest Cray is the Y-MP C-90.

It can be configured with up to 16 microprocessors, each capable of one gigaflop (a billion floating point operations) per second. With all 16 installed, then it is capable, theoretically, of 16 gigaflops; four times as fast as the previous model. It has a clock speed of something like 330 MHz. All that for just thirty million. I suppose the NSA gets a discount in lots of a dozen.

Another new model, the Y-MP EL, is a little more affordable. The EL can be configured with up to 4 CPU's and one thousand megabytes of memory. It runs something like 106 million floating point instructions per second with gusts up to 133. Price is from 300 thousand to about a million and a half. If enough people buy this book, I'll run out and get one.

Another supercomputer that was just unveiled last year is from Thinking Machines. It sells for about 30 million, and is capable of a trillion operations per second.

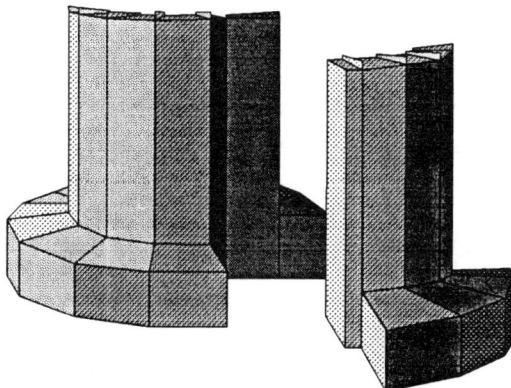

A computer generated drawing of the Cray-1 super computer. Completed in 1976, this number crunching monster took uo 70 sq feet of floor space, weighed 5 tons, and used 200,000 chips.

It generated so much heat that a "captive" cooling system was built in.

Originally selling for 15 million, they are being sold for scrap metal, and there is one in the Smithsonian museum.

THE DES FACT SHEET

Introduction

The National Institute of Standards and Technology (NIST) of the Department of Commerce has recently received many inquiries regarding various aspects of the Data Encryption Standard (DES).

This document addresses those frequently asked questions and provides interested individuals with sources of additional information. The document is not designed to issue new policy; rather it summarizes and clarifies existing policies. Additional guidance concerning the use of National Security Agency (NSA) developed Type II and Low-Cost Encryption Authentication Devices (LEAD) is planned to be issued in 1990.

Background

Issued as Federal Information Processing Standard Publication (FIPS PUB) 46 in 1977, the DES was promulgated by NIST (then the National Bureau of Standards) to provide a system for the protection of the confidentiality and integrity of the federal government's sensitive unclassified computer information. FIPS PUB 46 is based upon work by the International Business Machines Corporation and has been approved as American National Standard X3.92-1981/R1987. The DES has been reaffirmed twice, most recently in 1988. The current standard, which was issued as FIPS PUB 46-1, reaffirms the standard until 1993.

Technical Overview

The Data Encryption Standard specifies a cryptographic algorithm that converts plaintext to ciphertext using a key, a process called encryption. The same algorithm is used with the same key to convert ciphertext back to plaintext, a process called decryption. The DES consists of 16 "rounds" of operations that mix the data and key together is a prescribed manner using the fundamental operations of permutation and substitution. The goal is to completely scramble the data and key so that every bit of the ciphertext depends on every bit of the data and every bit of the key (a 56-bit quantity for the DES). After sufficient "rounds" with a good algorithm, there should be no correlation between the ciphertext and either the original data or key.

The DES uses 16 rounds for several reasons. First, a minimum of 12 rounds were needed to sufficiently scramble the key and data together; the others provided a margin of safety. Second, the operation of 16 rounds would return the key back to its original position in an electronic device for the next use when used in accordance with the published algorithm. Third, numerous "rounds" were needed to keep an analyst or adversary from working simultaneously forward and backward and "meeting in the middle" with a solution.

Security Provided by DES

The security provided by the DES depends on several factors: mathematical soundness, length of key, key management, input data formatting, mode of operation, implementation, application and threat.

The DES was developed to protect unclassified computer data in federal computer systems against a number of passive and active attacks in communications and storage systems. It was assumed that a knowledgeable person might seek to comprise the security system with resources commensurate to the value of the information to be obtained. Applications included Electronic Funds Transfer, privacy protection of personal information, personal authentication, password protection, access control, etc.

The DES has been evaluated by several organizations and has been determined to be mathematically sound. The effective length of the data key (56-bits) was challenged by several people as being too short for high security applications. Several people have analyzed the algorithm and have concluded that the algorithm is sound but would not be "if only this simple change was made." The most recent charge was that "if the DES has only 6 or 8 rounds instead of 16, then it could be broken on a personal computer in 0.3 seconds and 3 minutes respectively.

The two algorithms that were "broken on a personal computer" in 0.3 seconds and 3 minutes respectively WERE NOT THE DES. There is only one DES and any change to it results in an algorithm that IS NOT THE DES. Cryptographically, any algorithm that is obtained by any change to the DES may be significantly different in the security it provides. Thus, while the DES is sound, many algorithms that are similar to, but different from, the DES are not sound.

NIST has determined that at least until 1993, the DES will continue to provide more than adequate security for its intended applications. It is currently the only cryptographic method to be used in the federal government to protect unclassified computer data (except that information described in 10 U.S.C. Section 2315). However, NIST does plan to augment the DES with other cryptographic algorithms in a family of standards that will provide other types of protection in special applications (e.g., digital signatures, key exchange, exportable security). NIST will continue to support the use of DES in government security applications for the foreseeable future.

FIPS PUB 81, DES Modes of Operation

FIPS PUB 81 defines four modes of operation for DES which may be used in a wide variety of applications. The modes specify how data will be encrypted and decrypted. The four modes are:

(1) Electronic Codebook (ECB)
(2) Cipher Block Chaining (CBC)
(3) Cipher Feedback (CFB)
(4) Output Feedback (OFB).

For further information regarding other aspects of NIST's computer security program, including NIST's federal agency assistance program, please contact:

Computer Security Division
National Computer Systems Laboratory
Building 225, Room A216
National Institute of Standards and Technology
Gaithersburg, MD 20899
Telephone (301) 975-2934

HOW THE XOR WORKS

The exclusive or (XOR) is a type of logic gate or switch, used in digital electronics circuits and computer programs.

It is easier to understand the XOR by first knowing about two of the other types of gates, and how they work. These are the **AND** gate, and the **OR** gate.

An AND gate is like two (or more) switches inside a little box; switch A and switch B, which are used to turn a lamp on and off.

In the AND gate, these two switches are in series; one is after the other. For the lamp to turn **on**, both switches, A *and* B have to be turned **on**.

The OR gate is like two switches in parallel. If either switch A *or* switch B (or both) is turned **on** the lamp will turn **on**.

An XOR gate is different in that for the lamp to turn on, **one** of the switches, either switch A *or* switch B, must be turned **on**, but not *both* switch A *and* switch B.

Now how this relates to data encryption. Remember that the data the computer processes is in binary form, ones and zeros. As the computer looks at the data presented to it, that's what it sees: ones and zeros. In this illustration, a one is **on** and a zero is **off**.

These ones and zeros are called "bits". In order for these bits to mean anything, they are used in groups of eight, which are called "bytes". A byte is a single character; letter, digit, punctuation mark, etc.

So one of these bytes is seen by the computer as, for example, 10001001, which it recognizes as a character.

In the XOR process, as used in the DES CBC mode, two bytes are presented to the computer. One from the first block of plaintext, and one from the IV.

Suppose the first two bytes were 10001001 and 11000110. The first two bits are both ones, so the output of the XOR gate is a zero. The second two are a one and a zero, so the output is a one. Which Truth Table goes with which gate?

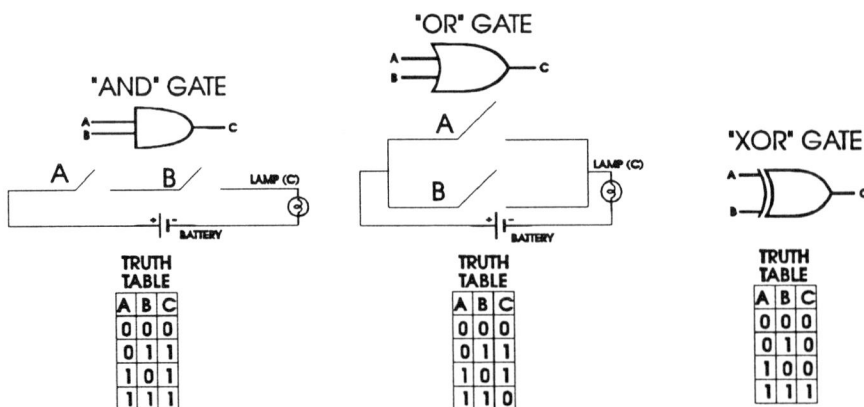

"AND" GATE

A	B	C
0	0	0
0	1	1
1	0	1
1	1	1

"OR" GATE

A	B	C
0	0	0
0	1	1
1	0	1
1	1	0

"XOR" GATE

A	B	C
0	0	0
0	1	0
1	0	0
1	1	1

ALSO FROM LYSIAS PRESS

WIRELESS MICROPHONES & SURVEILLANCE TRANSMITTERS

"The Bug Book". A detailed and comprehensive book on RF transmitters, "bugs". Sections include: "Who's (bugging) Who?"; "Hey, I'm on the Radio"; A few terms; Truth in advertising; The Bull in the Biz; Types of transmitters and trade-off's; Frequency coverage; How far will they *really* transmit?; All about antennas; The secret lives of batteries; Electronics 105; Applications for transmitters; How to install a surveillance transmitter; Receivers; Questions, answers, and comments; How to find a surveillance transmitter; What to do when you do find one; The physical search; Using "bug detectors"; An exercise in surveillance; The law; Some bugs reviewed including the VT-75; a new crystal controlled model for under $100 that is about to go on sale, and a new surface mount type with outstanding audio sensitivity; Bugs: the next generation; Big Brother is listening; Suggested reading; Places to get things; Glossary of terms. 8 1/2 by 11, 128 pages, illustrated.

Added just before it was sent to the printer is a section on court ordered surveillance, which has statistics for the last 11 years. Charts and graphs show the number of surveillance installations, the crime suspected, types of equipment used, which states had to most surveillance and other interesting information.

DON'T BUG ME

Don't Bug Me is an overview of electronic surveillance that covers all known methods of spying; hidden microphones, wiretapping, lasers, microwave, infrared and RF transmitters, etc. In addition, there are chapters on how to defend yourself against these methods of surveillance, and how to deal with those would spy on you.

Don't Bug Me has lots of charts and tables, illustrations and photographs, a bibliography and glossary of terms. 8 1/2 by 11. 140 pages. It is published by, and available from, Paladin Press. Single copies are available from Lysias Press for $20 plus $4.00 for first class postage. California residents, please add sales tax.

A number of other books are in the works. Some details are in The Bug Book. If you would like more information about them, write to Lysias Press.

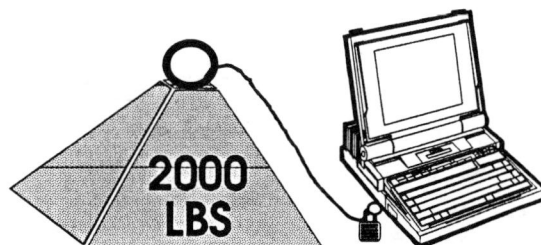

GLOSSARY OF TERMS

ADDRESS: To send E-Mail to someone you have to know their address just as you do to send paper mail. See the section on the Internet for more about this.

ALGORITHM: A way of solving a problem or making math calculations; a program or a set of instructions.

ARCHIVE: Another name for compressing a file into a smaller space so it takes up less room on the disk and can be transferred through electronic mail in less time. There are a number of utility programs that will compress a file, such as PKZIP, LZH, and ARJ.

ASCII: Acronym for the *American Standard Code for Information Interchange.* A set of ones and zeros used to represent letters and numbers, and other special characters.

ATTACK: To attempt to break or crack an encryption code or a message encrypted with the code. See also Brute Force, Trickery, and DFO.

BINARY: A method of counting based on the number 2 rather than 10; the "digits" used are ones and zeros as in the definition of **ASCII.** The binary equivalents for the numbers 0 through 15 are:

DEC	BIN	DEC	BIN
00	00	08	1000
01	01	09	1001
02	10	10	1010
03	11	11	1011
04	100	12	1100
05	101	13	1101
06	110	14	1110
07	111	15	1111

The pattern is easy to follow; converting from base ten to base two is easy.

BIOS: Basic Input/Output System. A routine or set of commands that allow a computer to communicate with its operating system. Usually contained inside a chip, the BIOS contains information on how the system is configured (the type and number of drives, type of monitor, etc) and the location of the operating system (which drive it is on) so the computer can find it. When a computer is first turned on, it reads this information (called initialization) then the operating system (DOS, OS-2, Unix, etc) takes over.

BIT: See also BINARY. A bit is one binary number or digit, based on the binary system of counting; a bit is a ONE or a ZERO. Ones and zeros are the "language" that a computer actually uses when it does something. Every program, every instruction, is made up of ones and zeros.

BOOT: Start. To turn on a computer so you can use it is to "boot" it.

BRUTE FORCE: Attempting to break a code by trying all of the possible keys in the DES, or factoring prime numbers in the RSA.

BYTE: Eight bits; one character; letter, number, etc.

CIPHER BLOCK CHAINING: One of the modes of the DES cipher; the most secure.

CIPHERTEXT: An encrypted message or file.

COMPLIANCE TEST: A self test built into the DES used to make sure it is operating correctly and has not been modified in any way.

CRASH: A situation in which a computer suddenly stops the program it was running, and does something wierd. It may drop back to the operating system or just freeze, so that it has to be rebooted, or reset. Very common in Microsoft Windows.

CSNET: Computer Science Network, one of the nets linked by the Internet.

CURSOR: The little blinking dot or square on the monitor screen that shows where the next character will *probably* appear.

CYBERSPACE: Cyberspace has been defined as the sum total of all of the computers and all of the networks that are connected together.

DECRYPTION: The reverse of encryption; decoding a scrambled message or file back into plaintext.

DFO: Damn Foolish Operator, someone who, among other things, uses easy to guess passwords, doesn't use secure erase, etc.

DIFFERENTIAL CRYPTANALYSIS: One method of attacking a cipher, based on making changes in the encrypted text and analyzing the result.

DOMAINS: Name given to different divisions or classifications of computers; *entities*, that are part of the Internet. Some of these are GOV (government); EDU (educational institutions) MIL (military) and COM (commercial).

DOWNLOAD: To receive a file from another computer.

DROP CARRIER: An impolite way to log off a BBS or database by entering the hangup command, rather than following the prompts.

EFF: Electronic Frontier Foundation.

ELECTRONIC CODE BOOK: One of the DES modes; the least secure.

ESS: Electronic Switching System, the present method used by telco to connect one phone to another, among many other things. ESS replaced the mechanical crossbar and stepping switch methods used many years ago, except for a few small independent telcos.

ENCRYPTION: The process of scrambling or encrypting plaintext into ciphertext.

EXCLUSIVE-OR (XOR) One type of digital electronic gate or switch. Others are AND, OR, NAND, NOR, & INVERTER. Also the process of using XOR logic to encrypt a file.

EXECUTABLE PROGRAM: A program that can be loaded into a computer and used (executed) by typing in (usually) the program name. In other words, it is ready to use as is. Also a program that deserves to be executed, such as Windows. Sorry, but I couldn't resist that one.

EXPANSION SLOT: A connector on a computer motherboard for plugging in other circuit boards.

FACTORING: Factoring means reducing a number to the set of primes that were multiplied together to produce it. For example 15 would factor to 3 and 5.

FAT: File Allocation Table. The FAT is a 'record keeping' file (actually there are two of them, in case one should become corrupted) that keeps track of the files on a disk. Hard disk or floppy disk. The FAT tells the system where on the disk a file is located so that it can be found, and how much space is free or available for use. See also SECURE ERASE

FLAME: A sometimes heated argument or discussion on one of the Internet's USENET newsgroups, or private BBS.

FIPS: Federal Information Processing Standard. Tekkie stuff on government standards for computers and programming and like that.

FTP: File Transfer Protocol. Any of a number of ways data is transferred from one computer to another.

GARBAGE: Random, meaningless characters on a computer screen, the result of something going wrong. Also similar characters received in data transmission caused by noise or interference on a phone line, or LAN.

HEXADECIMAL: (HEX) Another method of counting based on the number 16. It uses the digits 0 to 9 and then the letters A through F. Not as easy to understand as binary.

INTERNET: A computer data communications network that links a number of other networks. There are hundreds of these nets. It is an international system that ties many thousands of different individual computers of all types, together. This includes mainframes, mini's and PC's, DOS and Mac, UNIX and VAX, all of which can communicate with each other and send electronic mail and files back and forth.

KEYSPACE: Another term for key length.

LAN: Local Area Network. A LAN is a system of computers or peripherals connected together. This can be as simple as two computers sharing one printer, or as complex as dozens of terminals accessing a central data storage area. Where LAN's originally used wires or cables, many of them are now using infrared or microwave transmissions.

LANGUAGE: (Computer languages) Any of various sets of instructions that allow humans to communicate with computers, often against the wishes of said computers. Fortran (FORmula TRANslation) BASIC, "C", Pascal, COBOL, and Assembly are examples of languages. A computer program, any program, a word processor, spreadsheet, etc are written in one of these languages.

There is another language called %$*&#%@!!. which is for one way verbal communication with computers when they do unexpected or undesired things.

LOGICAL DRIVE: Partitions. Divisions or compartments of a hard disk drive that the computer, and the software it is running, see as if they were separate physical drives.

Logical drives are useful for organizing different types of files. One could, for example, place their word processor on logical drive C, their database on logical drive D, and their X-rated GIF files on logical drive E...

MENU DRIVEN: A program that lets the user select the things they want to do from a list (menu) rather than having to type them in from the command line.

MODEM: MOdulator DEModulator, a device that converts (modulates) computer data into audio for transmission over a LAN or phone line, and (demodulates) it, converts it back to computer data as it is received.

MOTHER BOARD: The main printed circuit board in a personal computer. It holds the microprocessor, memory, ROM, and a number of other chips. Also on the mother board are expansion slots into which various other printed circuit boards can be plugged. A driver for a printer and monitor, a modem, and like that.

NET: Network. Any of a number of ways that computers are connected together. Internet, Fidonet, Nikenet, LAN, WAN, are examples of networks.

NEWSGROUPS: Groups of Information, topics, on the Internet. There are something like 3000 of them, divided into various classes such as .sci (science), .rec (recreation), .soc (social issues) and .alt (alternative) which are alternative subjects.

NIKE NET: The name taken from the company that makes shoes, it is the process of hand delivering data by walking from one computer to another and carrying a floppy disk. Over short distances, it is the fastest, most efficient, most secure, and most error free method of data transfer known to exist.

NSFNET: The National Science Foundation Network.

PARALLEL: SERIAL and PARALLEL are the two ways in which data can move from one place to another. This can be within a computer, from a computer to peripheral devices such as a modem or a printer, or from one computer to another. In SERIAL transfer, the information flows one bit at a time through a single path (wire) like cars lined up on a one lane road. Parallel is like an 8 (or more) lane freeway, data flows 8 bits (or more) at a time. Parallel is much faster at moving data than serial, the same as the freeway moves cars faster than the one lane road.

PARITY: A method of error checking used with data transfer. Simplified explanation: It consists of counting the number of ones (or zeros) in a block of text, and comparing this number at the receiving end to make sure it is the same. If it is not, it indicates a probable error in transmission.

PATH: The directions used by the computer to find a particular file. If a file is named "mysecret.txt, and it is on drive C, and is in a subdirectory called "secrets", then the path would be C:\secrets\mysecret.txt.

PLAINTEXT: A message in plain English, (or other language) before it is encrypted.

PLAINTEXT-CIPHERTEXT PAIRS: A message, file, etc, in both clear and encrypted forms. By comparing the two, it is possible (though very difficult) to derive the key.

POINT OF FOOLISHNESS: (POOF) The point in the complexity of an encryption algorithm at which it could not be broken using predicted future technology and in-

creases in speed, within the probable life span of planet Earth.

POST: A message entered, posted, on a BBS or network. The act of posting a message.

PRIME NUMBER: A number that can be *evenly* divided only itself or one. Seven is a prime; it can be evenly divided only by 1 and seven. Eight is not a prime number as it can be evenly divided by 2 or 4 as well as 1 and 8.

PROTO BOARD: A proto board is system of one or more plastic strips, of varying size, that have rows of holes into which the wires (leads) of electronic components can be plugged. They are used to build prototypes of electronic circuits because the components can be quickly inserted and removed.

PUBLIC DOMAIN: Public domain software. A program that has been released for public use without charge. This may be with the condition that it is not modified, used commercially or resold for a profit. Like shareware, there are some excellent programs available.

REGISTER: A temporary storage place for data. When data comes into a computer, from the keyboard for example, it first goes to a register where it is held until the microprocessor receives another instruction telling it where to send that data; to RAM or a disk drive, etc.

RELATIVELY PRIME: Relatively prime means that if you factor two numbers they don't have any common prime factors. For example 12 and 15 are not relatively prime, since 12 factors as 2 * 2 * 3, and 15 factors as 3 * 5, and both of them have a 3. But 12 and 35 are relatively prime, since 35 factors as 5 * 7 and so there are no common prime factors.

RUPA: Requisite University Poor Acoustics. All universities have at least one large lecture hall where the acoustics are so bad that only the students in the first row can understand what the instructor is saying.

SCI.CRYPT: The science of cryptology. One of the newsgroups on the Internet. It contains commentary on the legal, social, and political aspects of data encryption, and information about the science itself.

SECURE ERASE: When you *delete* a file from a disk (hard or floppy) you are not actually erasing the file, you are telling another file on the disk, called the File Allocation Table (which is a record of the files on the disk) that the file is no longer needed. Then that space can be used for storing something else.

The complete, intact, file is still there until it is written over by another file. This might not happen for days or months, depending on how much free space is on the disk and how often you use it. Even then, some parts of it might remain.

A number of programs may be able to recover that file, the Norton Utilities for example. There are also programs known as *disk explorers*, with which one can go through the area where a deleted file remains and examine it a block or even one byte at a time, and possibly reconstruct it. Secure erase writes over the deleted file with random characters or zeros, depending on the program, so that it can **probably** never be recovered.

Most of the encryption programs listed here have secure erase, as does Norton Utilities, and XTree Gold, (an outstanding program) has a "diskwash" function to prevent erased files from being undeleted or recovered. However, it is possible that the weak traces of magnetism left on the disk from the secure erased file can be analyzed and recovered. The more passes used in secure erase, the less chance there is of this happening. See also the review of Encrypt-It.

SERIAL: See PARALLEL.

SHAREWARE: Shareware program. A computer program that is distributed free from BBS systems, or at low cost (usually $5.00 per disk or less) by shareware distributors and some retail computer stores.

The concept is that a person can try it out before they buy it. If they decide to keep and use it, they are required to pay a registration fee to the person who wrote it. There are thousands of shareware programs available, some of which are as good, or better, than commercial software.

SOURCE CODE: A computer program in it's original "plain English" form. In this form, it can be analyzed by a programmer to tell what the program is, what it does, and, in the case of an encryption program, if there are any trap doors or other sneak attack methods that could be used to break it.

SWITCH: One or more characters added to a command that modify what the command does. For example, when formatting a floppy disk in drive A (from DOS) one types in [format A:]. If you add "\s" [format A: /s] this tells DOS to copy the operating system to the disk after it is formatted. So [/s] is the switch.

SYSOP: System Operator. The person who operates a BBS.

SYSOP ACCESS: Having the same access to a BBS system as the sysop, usually from a remote computer. A person with such access can log on and have complete control over the system.

TAG: To select, or mark, certain files so as to be able to do an operation (erase or copy, for example) on all of them at once.

TELCO: The telephone company. Any telephone company.

TCP/IP: Transmission Control Protocol/Internet Protocol, two of a number of protocols used on the Internet.

TRAP DOOR: A secret routine built into a program that can be used to break into it. A weak prime number that is easily factored in the public key system.

TRICKERY: Any of several ways to break an encrypted file by anticipating and trying passwords, using dictionaries, etc.

TRUTH TABLE: A chart that lists all of the possible logic level inputs to a gate and the output based on them. See the illustration.

TSR: Terminate and Stay Resident, a program that is loaded into memory (RAM) and then remains there while the system is doing something else. When the operator wants to use the TSR they push two or so "hot keys". Since the program is already in RAM it works instantly, and they don't have to wait for it to load from the hard disk drive.

UART: Universal Asynchronous Receiver\Transmitter. A chip used in modems (and other devices) to send and receive data.

UNIX: UNIX is an operating system for large computers as DOS and OS-2 are operating systems for personal computers. UNIX is complex and very cryptic, and is difficult to learn, compared to DOS which is fairly easy. There are also "flavors" of Unix that run on personal computers.

UPLOAD: To send a file to another computer.

UUCP: [UUCP node] A computer system that can send and receive electronic mail on the Internet. Access to UUCP is available from some local, free, BBS's, or for a fee through The Well, Compuserve, etc. UUCP systems do not actually provide users direct access to the Internet.

WAN: Wide Area Network.